Live Well. Die Well.

Suffering and The Path Home

Live Well, Die Well

Suffering and Healing Early Hours

Live Well
Die Well

Suffering and The Path Home

G. R. Burns

Pacific Book Publishing
Seattle, WA

Other Books by G. R. Burns

Forged Through Fire: Developing Preparedness for the Perilous Encounter
The Bloodline of Kings: Days of Our Past
The Bloodline of Kings: An Ancient Prince

Copyright © 2024 G. R. Burns
All rights reserved
Cover Design © 2024 Melissa Burns
All rights reserved

Published 2024 by
Pacific Book Publishing, LLC
8911 Vernon RD STE 125, Lake Stevens WA, 98258
www.Pacific-Books.com

Printed in the United States of America

ISBN: 978-1-7373291-0-7

This edition contains all corrections and revisions that have been made since the original publication

*For those with buried pains and broken hearts.
Reality is hard. Answers are near.*

&

For the Strike Teams

CONTENTS

Live Well: a Prerequisite for Dying well   1

Logical Reasoning: The Crux of Worldview   17

Power and Complacency: The Birth of Relativism   34

Matter, Chance, and Science: Materialism   51

The Elements of Reality   67

Local Agency   78

The Agency of Origins   89

A Context for Trauma   107

Victory Guaranteed   117

Tactics For Living Well 1.0   131

Tactics For Living Well 2.0   142

It's Personal   161

Chapter One

Live Well: A Prerequisite for Dying Well

"You don't know what the F*** you're talking about."

The statement caught me by surprise. I had just finished teaching a day-long de-escalation training, which I always end with a short talk on personal recovery from violent trauma. Typically, everyone leaves a class slightly overwhelmed and entirely empowered, armed with new tools to prevent personal violence and improve many other aspects of their relationships. Not this guy. He was obviously trying to get a point across. But what point, exactly?

An insult is usually a distraction from a real problem lurking under the surface. When you are confronted like this, don't take it personally! *Especially* if it is a threat – veiled or direct – always ask a clarifying question. As a rule, when someone makes a statement *they* bear the burden of proof, and we tend to let people who make outrageous claims drive the conversation.[1] I wasn't planning on letting him off the hook, so I gave him a chance to develop his thought and take responsibility.

"I'm a little confused. What exactly do you mean?"

Responding with a calm, direct question caught this guy off guard. He smoothed his white hair back, with trembling hands, to buy himself time to think.

"You heard me. You don't know what it's like to have your loved ones die in front of you...I do! Four of my best friends died on my lap in the fields of Vietnam. You don't know what you're talking about."

Now we were getting somewhere, but he wasn't out of the hot seat yet.

"Well, you're right about that. I haven't been there. So, what would you say to a group like this if you had five minutes to teach them about recovery from violent trauma?"

Hmm. Eventually, the silence became awkward. His answer became apparent even before he mumbled:

"I don't know."

This is the problem. We don't know how to justify hard circumstances in the human condition (like death) with how we perceive reality. Experience devastates our principles, instead of re-enforcing them, plunging us into an unexpected whirlwind of suffering.

Trauma, though it comes in various forms, affects the human condition in an almost universal fashion.[2] Trauma results when an experience challenges or destroys a fundamental set of perceptions or principles by which we understand the world. The more foundational the set of principles destroyed, the greater the resulting trauma.

Consciously and subconsciously, we answer fundamental questions about reality and develop a *worldview*. We all have a worldview, a patchwork of culturally acquired notions, natural intuitions, early childhood experiences, and reactions to lessons learned. These harden into a paradigm, a frame of reference, a filter through which we see the world, make sense of reality, and stabilize our existence.

On a *worldview* we must build a *life*. With it we interpret our experience of *reality*.

But reality is big.

Bigger than anyone's perspective.

The weather of harsh experience tests our worldview like high winds test a forest of oaks. All are damaged. Some stand and heal. Some fall and rot.

We humans are all tested by experiences. We suffer injuries. We stand and heal; or we stand and cope, growing new bark over unhealed wounds which rot our hearts.

Sometimes we topple.

Thus, extreme trauma is the result of a test – a test of how a person's fundamental beliefs hold up to reality. When a person walks into a storm of experience with an immature, incomplete, or frankly incorrect worldview, the damage is often devastating. Recovery becomes extremely difficult, and the resulting trauma can form an emotional and psychological trap.

We are survivors.

Survivors do not always thrive.

To thrive requires a worldview which corresponds to reality.

Surprisingly, worldviews aren't consistently formed across a lifetime. They harden during key stages of development and are often shaped more by the 'tone' of our experiences, notions, and culture, than by objectively tested propositions.

The plasticity of the human brain is paradoxically both well-researched and barely understood.[3] For natural and social reasons, young children (estimated 0-3 years) and young adults (estimated 13-19 years) of all demographics have a propensity to explore, test boundaries, and make long-term conclusions about their perceived environment.[4] The worldview developed during these normal stages of plasticity is typically, once accepted, never significantly altered throughout life – even when the notions it is based upon are mutually contradictory, obviously inadequate, or demonstrably false.

Thus, many people live and function with an inaccurate or incomplete worldview, which lacks correct answers to key questions. Many people are ill prepared to consider the cost of extreme loss, killing, or being killed.

I am convinced this represents the majority of people, from all regions, religions, demographics, and socioeconomic statuses. When trauma strikes, the house of cards has a tendency to topple. All the way down.

Most worldviews don't stand up to reality.

When I was fifteen, I was in my first 'Active Killing' incident. I was in high school. I remember it being early morning. I was wearing shorts, despite the cold.

I was walking behind Joe and his new girlfriend, on my way to math class. I remember seeing her face: her mouth is open and she's screaming. I can't hear her screams when I remember the incident, however, because my heart rate was over a hundred and sixty beats per minute.

The scenes flash in and out within my mind.

Joe falling.

A concrete garbage can.

A PE teacher running against the massive tide of screaming kids.

Then...nothing, for days and weeks.

Joe was shot several times in the back by a fellow classmate named Vincent, in an act of targeted violence. Joe survived. He dropped out of school, got into hard drugs, and his world fell apart. Today, he is plagued by anxiety and constant pain.[5]

Vincent walked off campus and was talked out of committing suicide by a fellow TTA co-worker (and then police Hostage-Negotiator), Dave. Vincent was arrested. He went to jail. He analyzed his worldview. Now he has a wife and baby, and serves as a volunteer firefighter to try and save lives.

If we step back from the horror and apparent unfairness of this incident, we can see how unique trauma is. It provides a T in the road. Will the recipient of trauma cling to an incomplete worldview (and their trauma) for the rest of their life? Or will they rebuild on new principles? I had a choice. So did Joe and Vincent.

The choice isn't easy, and the circumstances that bring such a choice about are never fair. Rebuilding a worldview is a terribly demanding task, especially within the lonely dark of a traumatic event. It only becomes more daunting the older you are, and the more history you have within an incomplete worldview.

Left alone, suffering does not diminish with time. It deepens, seeping into other memories, infecting relationships, and destroying life.

Of course, it's best to prevent this fork in the road from occurring at all, by simply establishing a correct worldview to begin with. 'Simple' isn't the right word though. Raising children isn't simple. Being a teenager isn't simple. Being a human isn't simple.

How can an adult regain the plasticity necessary to analyze and recreate their worldview? Trauma can initiate the open-mindedness necessary to think deeply and objectively. Screaming, clawing, life-rending experience savagely juxtaposes a coddled personal perception with an unflinching reality. After the crisis of a traumatic event, the failure of said *worldview* to explain *life* can become devastatingly obvious. In the ashes of a life broken physically, emotionally, relationally, and psychologically, questions arise.

People can be resilient, but we would be fools to wait around for the next traumatic event in our lives to update our worldview. There is a safer, more manageable way to increase plasticity in adults. I stumbled upon it, seemingly by accident, while training and studying emergency preparedness, trauma, and recovery.

For thousands of years, professional combat entities like Sparta's Hoplites, Napoleon's Grande Armée, Britain's Commando Units, and U.S. Special Forces have been inducing controlled levels of trauma as a means to teach automatic brain function, and the character necessary to survive and excel in dangerous environments. Controlled tactics training, and especially stress inoculation training, increases the natural plasticity of the participants. The primary result is the ability to perform better under stress.[6]

A secondary, and less-looked for result, is an ability to analyze previously held, and subsequently fractured, concepts. Stress inoculation training is a perfect environment to challenge false views of reality.

Unfortunately, most professional combat entities seem to focus on stress inoculation and combat readiness, ignoring the potential for correcting inaccurate worldviews and equipping warriors to thrive post-mission. Perhaps they aren't aware how important correct principles are to recovering after a traumatic event. Perhaps they don't care, or don't want to touch the aspect of *worldview* for fear of liability...or coming across as narrow-minded.

Ten years into my emergency preparedness journey, I began taking this seriously with those I was training. The result was our Strike Team program at the Tactical Training Academy. We invite participants to go far beyond training to kill or be killed. We require a systematic evaluation of their worldview. This teamwork program guides trainees into a state of intellectual rigor and psychological plasticity, where it is possible for them to make powerful, life-influencing choices; to learn to live deliberately and face death with courage and honor.

These strike teams conduct force-on-force based training in almost every environment you can think of: houses, forests, darkness, in and around vehicles, on the ground, with and without firearms, etc. They are stabbed with taser knives, shot with less-lethal ammunition, and prepared to withstand the trauma of emergency events and combat. They get cold, hungry, hot, and tired. They work together, sweat together, and problem-solve together in managed-stress scenarios. But they do more: they write letters to their children, they read challenging material with their spouses, they share their weaknesses with trusted friends, and they seek a Truth not based on personal perspective or cultural fads. They analyze their principles with open eyes.

And they grow.

Together.

The results are astonishing. Over the course of the program, participants begin to develop an objectively testable, deeply-held worldview; open-ended enough to allow growth, and correspondent enough to withstand extreme trauma. Traumatic events, in fact, cease to be the defining aspect in their lives, and become another experience to grow through.

Trauma seems to lose its power.

It starts to disappear.

Traumatic events highlight the incongruity between reality and the worldview most people live with.

Doing the hard work of developing a truth-correspondent worldview prepares us to withstand trauma and to live well. Right-thinking is prerequisite to resilience, long-term healing, and recovery.

Living well prepares us to face death well – the death of others, and each person's own inevitable death. If you are training to face death in self-defense, law enforcement, combative training, emergency medicine, search and rescue, and other high-stakes endeavors, you cannot neglect the prerequisite of living well.

Apathy and an internally inconsistent worldview are more dangerous than the trauma which reveals them. People who witness or participate in a lethal force encounter are three times more likely to die of suicide than they are to be killed in a violent event.[7] We lose more vets to suicide, drug overdoses, and alcohol abuse than in combat – twenty-five times as many, to be precise.[8] What we carry inside must be more dangerous than the bullets that fly.

Our culture is saturated with killing, yet we neglect formally discussing the principles upon which life is based. Is it any surprise, then, that life falls to pieces after a real traumatizing event?

I train people to kill and to die. Some trainers don't like this terminology, preferring watered-down terms that assist with dehumanizing the opponent

Begged me.

Again and again, over and over, he pleaded: "Kill me. Please!" He believed his life was not worth living and never would be.

When I was younger and my worldview merely an untried, tenuous philosophy, I may have agreed with his conclusion. Now, as I've trained and lived and asked hard questions about what is right, I have spent less time training to kill and more time training to live well.

You may ask why a person like Austin deserves saving. It is a reasonable question. He asked it, and couldn't find a good answer.

Of course, the answer depends on your worldview. Is there a worldview where saving lives *and* taking them can be justifiable? Honorable? Right? How will you know the difference?

Avoiding the question, though the most common solution, is not the right answer.

As I turned over custody of Austin, he looked me hard in the face and said, "I've *never* had a man talk to me..." he choked up, and then continued, "...like you have."

I don't know if Austin ever actually took a hard look at his life and principles. I do know he was given the choice to do so. I gave him that choice. Doing so aligned with *my* principles, my worldview.

Was I traumatized by this event? Did my family have to sell our house and move, to try and forget what happened? Do my children wake up in the middle of the night, screaming as they relive the event within the trapped confines of their mind?

No.

On the contrary, our family looks back on that day with fondness. It was a good day. In fact, it was one of the best days we have had in our home. This is no exaggeration. Reality tested our worldview. The result was the absence of burden, suffering, and trauma. Instead, we simply felt alive, like the world made sense.

Do you see how this would have been substantially different if our worldview didn't align with reality? It's strong evidence that whatever principles my family is building our life on are the *right* ones. They correspond to a truth that is bigger than we are.

Don't think that I'm overlooking the real physiological and emotional fall-out that occurs after a stress-induced endorphin dump (particularly one that occurs during a use of force). I have measured this fallout in my bodily system to the day and hour post-incident. It is a reality that happens, and is discussed in later chapters.

There is a difference between *physiological backlash* and *trauma*. The first is like a bruise, it occurs under certain conditions and then fades (from my experience after about 48 hours. It is the same measured timeline whether I am recovering a body or recovering from a use of force). The second is like bruising that turns into a clot, which then lodges in your heart or your head, causing suffering for the rest of your life – fracturing your relationships, your communication, and eventually leading to your death.

We must have an accurate worldview to live well.

We must live well to die well.

This book proceeds like a guide: it briefly articulates some worldviews common in our culture today, analyzes each with rational thinking and, I hope, leads you toward principles that will withstand trauma and dark times.

Now, for a warning. I am not a psychologist, but I find the justification of violence within human cultures to be categorically similar. I am not a philosopher, but I question agency in the world, look to the laws of causality, and find the intricacies of infinitude to be consistent – and mind boggling. I am not a physicist, but I think the effects of dark energy on the expansion of the universe are fascinating. I am not a theologian, but I see that the fractals of history unfold toward a destination. I have asked questions and sought out good answers.

In the end, my argument is pretty simple: if your worldview doesn't align with reality, you're a liability on the battlefield, in your relationships, and in your home. If you're training to kill or be killed, and you're not taking the time to consider the implications of how your principles align with the real world, you are asking to become a casualty. Perhaps worst of all, if you are not choosing to live your daily life aligned with the facts of how things really are, the casualties will occur in your home, in your relationships, and in the depths of your heart.

Facing death well requires a choice – it is a choice to live well, to live aligned with the reality of the world.

What We Learned in this Chapter:

Traumatic events test our worldview against reality. Great trauma correlates with a misunderstanding of reality, an inadequate worldview, stunting a person's ability to recover and thrive.

Thus, to mitigate and recover from trauma, we must see the world as it really is and live accordingly. However, worldviews are difficult to change within adults. The neurological and psychological plasticity necessary to develop, question, and adopt worldviews (which are naturally occurring in children), are typically inadequate and are rarely altered into adulthood. This leaves many adults unable to cope with and recover from traumatic events.

The plasticity to re-engage with fundamental questions typically occurs after a serious traumatic event exposes holes in a worldview. Alternatively, stress-induced combat training, with the correct guidance, creates a safer, more manageable opportunity for adult plasticity.

This book is written as a guide for those ready to honestly question why key elements of their lives, beliefs, and relationships do not function under pressure. Establishing a worldview that corresponds to reality is a necessary foundation for combat training, raising children, loving a spouse, and living a generous, full, abounding LIFE. Which, in turn, allows us to face death with courage.

Preparing to withstand and recover from trauma requires a life aligned with reality.

Chapter One Notes

[1] Gregory Koukl, *Tactics*. Grand Rapids: Zondervan, 2009. This book is an invaluable resource that expands on this methodology.

[2] American Psychiatric Association, *Diagnostic and Statistical Manual of Mental Disorders*. 5th ed., Text Revision, American Psychiatric Publishing, 2022.

[3] Vanessa Burns et al., *Neuronal Dynamics Regulating Brain and Behavioral State Transitions*. Cell, 2019. Yes, for those of you paying attention: this is my sister.

[4] Laurance Steinberg, *Age of Opportunity: Lessons from the new science of adolescence.* Boston, New York: Houghton, Mifflin, Harcourt, 2014.

[5] The Washington Post, *Victim of 2006 school shooting in Roseburg, Ore., tormented by latest casualties*. October, 2015.

[6] Daniel Kahneman, *Thinking, Fast and Slow*. New York: Farrar, Straus and Giroux, 2011.

[7] National Tactical Officers Association. Regional SWAT Team Active Shooter Training, 2018.

[8] US Defense Casualty Analysis System and the US Department of Veteran Affairs. Data from 2001-2021. Active duty and veteran service member suicides are combined.

Chapter Two

Logical Reasoning: The Crux of Worldview

Nearly every resource I come across for preventing, mitigating, and responding to trauma fails to keep its worldview straight. One book takes a hack at religion, pointing out that it doesn't align with evolutionary theories, and then justifies its argument based on objective morality (by saying, for example, "It's not *right* that people in power take advantage of the weak..."). One psychologist swipes at objective morality, stating that whatever a person feels must be right, and then they produce evidence to help you feel the way "you ought to feel" (which made me feel like they were wrong. So...were they?). A religious leader jabs at scientific theory, pointing to some groundbreaking scientific geological evidence to validate their claim.

You see the problem. We're surrounded by opinions of what reality is like. If we're going to make any progress to find real answers, we need to get our story straight. And keep it that way.

Thus, before we start asking what the truth is, we must determine *how* to think, ask questions, and develop sound answers. We must learn how to *keep* our story straight before we start looking at the details of the story in question.

Thinking well is called logical reasoning. It provides a basket that truth can be collected within. If you have holes in your basket, you can't be sure that what you put in there will stay.

It is confusing and upsetting when logical reasoning is absent from conclusions. Those conclusions won't make any sense. It is terrifying how often this occurs within our culture, at every level, and in every medium. I come across the absence of logical thinking in regular conversation and in audio, visual, and published sources.

The other day, my kids and I were reading the *Inheritance Cycle*, by Christopher Paolini. I was startled as an old elf, called Oromis, delivered so-called "wisdom" to the main character (and, therefore, to my children who were reading).

On one hand he asserts that, "[what is right and wrong] depends upon how you choose to view the world." That is quite a claim. Suddenly, he is claiming something else: "We stand between the light and the dark, and keep the balance between the two..." A few pages later, he makes another claim: "[Without god] it is a better world. A place where we are responsible for our own actions, where we can be kind to one another because we want to and because it is the right thing to do."

Oromis can't see it, but he's setting himself up for

a serious dilemma. Do you see the logical problem? Is "rightness" *relative*, stemming from inside a personal view and nothing more? Or is it *objective*, an existing standard to which all are ultimately measured? Oromis claims that there is no evil, just perspective. Then he immediately contradicts his narrative, interposing himself between real light and real darkness.

Which is it?

Each of these claims stem from a worldview much older than Oromis. The first is called relativism. The next, dualism. The third, atheism. They don't play well together. When trauma comes, this house is going to collapse with a bang.

Sure, this is a fiction novel. We don't need to poke holes in this fictional world. We *do* need to help our children see the problem: a world can't exist, even a fictional one, without logical consistency. It would be one thing if Paolini's character was designed to be a confused, disoriented, and slightly crazed recluse living among creatures de-evolving into animals. On the contrary, this character is portrayed as a sage of deep wisdom, the epitome of an entire race. It echoes the confusion saturating our culture.

"Logic will never fail you," Oromis claims. I wish he would have stopped there. He might be right, but at this point I don't trust him. He seems incapable of knowing what logic is. He doesn't keep his story straight.

Neither do we.

I have an acquaintance that we will call Phil. Phil once conveyed to me his conviction that a large, intelligent creature (whom he called Bigfoot) was in active existence near the area that consists of my backyard. This was a startling claim to make. As you can probably guess, it was time for me to figure out his reasons. He had some.

Phil articulated to me how, while on a remote hike nearby, he had come across a series of trees that had large strips of bark, approximately four inches wide by twenty feet long, stripped vertically from the trees. He excitedly showed me a picture.

"Look at this," he exclaimed, his eyes beaming. "This isn't natural. Something did this. And look at this..." he paused, swiping to a new picture. "I found one of the strips of bark all wound up nearby. I got it back to my rig. I'm going to take it down to a university to see if they can find any saliva samples on it."

This is quite an assertion, with pictures to prove it. When reasons for a view are presented, we should identify if those reasons are *logical*: possible, probable, and likely – all while avoiding contradiction. I took a good look at his picture.

"Well, this certainly isn't natural, I'll give you that," I admitted, looking closely at the picture. "Look at the bottom of the bark here, that's a clean-cut line with ninety-degree angles, and you can see a scar left in the soft wood. It's clearly made by an object with a straight, hard edge that was pressed directly into the tree. Like an ax."

Phil nodded, even more excited, and started going off on a tangent about how Bigfoot could use metal tools and more, like transfer in and out of the space time continuum to avoid detection. I gently brought him back to the first claim. There is no sense moving on to a new link in a chain of reasoning, when the first link hasn't been developed.

"Phil," I asked gently, "what makes you think Bigfoot is the best explanation of this? Have you looked at any other possibilities?"

He emphatically shook his head up and down. He had done the research. There was no other option.

Or had he?

Unfortunately for Phil, my wife was sitting nearby. During the span of our conversation, she had pulled up her phone and done a quick Google search regarding what Phil had found. She interjected softly.

"I think you should probably take a look at this."

Phil's eye's narrowed as he looked at several images of trees that looked like the ones he had found, with piles of wound-up bark that looked like the one he had acquired.

"Where did you find this?" he whispered.

"It's a local Native American bark-weaving group," explained my wife. "Looks like they meet out at that exact trail every other Thursday."

Phil blinked, then didn't hesitate.

"Well, look at this..." and he immediately produced another woodland phenomenon that he used to justify his conclusions about Bigfoot. After three or four rounds of this, I had to simply end the conversation.

Before we seek out reality, we need to be able to determine *when* we find it.

Logical reasoning is the foundation of human society. Think about it. Every human worldview assumes it's the correct one for reasons. When a person makes a claim, they typically have a reason for doing so or, at least, they should have one (and they *know* they should have one). No reasonable person takes a claim seriously, when there are no reasons to support the claim!

Humans rely on reasoning as a prerequisite for every other conceived conclusion about reality. Future conclusions build on historical ones. Reasoning is like an anchor. Each link in an anchor chain is vital to keeping the ship grounded. In short, nothing makes sense...unless some things make sense.

As we have already identified, the problem is that most people have little desire to examine every chain-link in their worldview; until the chain snaps, and they are floating adrift. The result is a worldview-chain composed of various principles and beliefs that don't attach anywhere – not even to each other.

Logical reasoning is based on a simple principle: if there are reasons for a cause or effect that make sense, the cause or event is probably true. If there are no reasons, or those reasons are impossible, implausible, or unlikely (for example, if those reasons contradict other necessarily true claims), then that link (and the corresponding worldview) doesn't make sense.

Generally speaking, this is called the assumption of the basic reliability of the senses,[1] and it assumes several factors you likely take for granted day-to-day because this assumption is necessary to make sense of even the most simple realities. When you have good reasons to believe you're in a forest, you can reasonably assume that there *is* a forest. If I say there is a circle and then tell you it is made of two parallel lines, you know I'm confused. If you throw a rock and it doesn't hit the ground, you know something *else* happened. It's basic logic.

This isn't to say human senses are infallible (an argument obviously proven false through experience - there would be no need for a book like this if it was so). We make mistakes about our reality all the time. Even though we make mistakes, it doesn't follow that we can't determine *any* elements of objective reality. Most instruments we use – calculators, telescopes, radar, night vision, etc. – improve our sense of fact. They don't contradict facts. When they do, we know they are broken and need fixing.

So, we can safely assume that logical thinking results in reasonable conclusions about the reality of how things are. Without basic logical assumptions, you can't even disagree (you'd be assuming too many facts)!

Notice, logical thinking involves a few elements:
1. A claim.
2. Reasons to support that claim.
3. Reasons that are reasonable: possible, plausible, and likely – all of which avoid contradiction.

Let's think logically for a minute about the following claim by using a basic logical formula:

Example A
Claim: The world is round.
You ask for reasons: What makes you think that's true?
Reasons: Gravity pulls massive objects into circular shapes due to the nature of mass equally affecting all sides of the object. The earth is a massive object; therefore, the earth is circular.
Follow-up: Does gravity do this consistently with all supermassive objects? If so, how do you know?

Example B
Claim: The world is round
You ask for reasons: What makes you think that's true?
Reasons: Everyone thinks the earth is round, are you crazy?
Follow-up: Well, I might agree that the earth is round – but I'm a little confused how my mental state has anything to do with how you came to that conclusion. Are you saying that the earth is round merely because everyone believes that? Does everyone believe that? What reasons are there for the majority to think the way they do?

Let's look at the key elements of logical reasoning.

First, notice the emphasis on how important it is to adopt logical reasoning as a daily habit. When someone makes a claim, they bear the burden of proof. Ask people for the reasons they have for a given view as a matter of practice, even if you agree. If you don't ask for reasons, no logical process takes place, unless it is occurring in the relative safety of your own mind. Going through this internal dialogue is possible and useful, of course, but engaging with people is a necessary element of reality. When you let other people get away with conclusions that don't have good reasons, you're apt to do so yourself.

Second, it must be apparent how even a basic claim requires many other claims to be necessarily true. Formally, this is called the law of causality.[2] There is a chain of reasoning: one link in the chain reasonably supports the next. In Example A, the person making the claim is asserting some facts about things that are not exactly the object in question. Namely, in this case, gravity, mass, and physics. How these principles interact all play a key role in determining the validity and soundness of the claim.

This evidence-based layout of logical reasoning provides an ample array of tests to verify if a claim is actually true. We can simply examine one link in a line of reasoning at a time, to see if the chain of a worldview fits with the facts of how things are.

You'll notice, however, that the legwork of this should be carried out by the person who holds the view. It is common in our culture to get responses that try to shift the burden of proof onto someone who didn't make the initial claim. Responses like Example B, "Oh, so you're one of those flat-earth people. What makes *you* think the earth is flat?" are prime examples. Don't let someone pass the buck, trying to get you to give reasons for *their* view! Politely remind the person you haven't shared what you think, you're simply asking for the reasons *they* have for what they've shared.

Third, it must be apparently obvious how exasperating this can be to a person who hasn't thought through their reasons, and is rather unwilling to engage in challenging their own comfortable, already-accepted worldview. It is exceptionally important, as you begin to think logically and engage others in this way, that you remain patient and genuinely curious. It will be startling how often people don't have reasons for what they think.

So, logical reasoning requires the ability to ask questions, ask follow-up questions, and be somewhat persistent when engaging with others.

We must also use this as a blueprint for the questions we ask ourselves. Do we have reasons that make logical sense, or are we spouting off what we read in a textbook or heard on the radio? Do our reasons link together coherently, like a chain, or are we wandering all over the place with our line of thinking?

Do you have logical reasons for what you think?

I rather unwillingly listened to a podcast where I heard an author suggest that it was a good idea to be "conspiracy minded". Of course, I didn't have an opportunity to ask exactly what he meant or his reasons for thinking the way he did. Nonetheless, I safely assumed (based on the content of the podcast) that he was suggesting people not only question what is true, but intentionally look for views that don't make much sense. Even if obvious, reasonable conclusions exist elsewhere.

This is ridiculous and dangerous.

The premise of 'question everything' is perfectly logical, and I agree wholeheartedly. But we must retain the ability to *accept* logical conclusions when they reasonably appear, and continue that retention until a more logical conclusion takes shape. Not doing so has a name: bias (confirmation bias, in this case).

Phil's claim about Bigfoot was based on a real reason. Yet, he didn't take the time to examine his reasons. When a proof appeared highly improbable, he immediately replaced that reason for another one, just as improbable. I think this is being "conspiracy minded", but I am going to call it foolishness. This strain of thought exists in almost every worldview on the planet.

Don't be a fool. If you neglect logical reasoning, you'll look like one, no matter your worldview – or, even worse, you'll be one. This is not a slight, it is a serious warning. Fools are not always silly, often they are dangerous. If you are not thinking clearly, a fool can weave a web of complexities that simply aren't true, leading many uneducated (or lazy) people into deception. Worse, they can start to teach you how to think *poorly* instead of logically.

I recommend gently correcting such thinkers and, if they persist, keeping them at an arm's length.

Logical reasoning is a necessary tool to possess before building the rest of the worldview boat, if you want it to float. Once grasped, it is time to start looking for sound claims and solid worldviews.

Some claims, of course, are stronger than others. Some principles are closer to the truth than others. Some worldviews are more accurate than others.

Now, if you're thinking logically, you might notice I just made a claim: that there is a right way to think, and that there are right answers (and, therefore, wrong ones). Well, if you're asking why I think that's true, ask yourself this: if you don't agree that some views are more accurate than others, is that conclusion (your view) more accurate than the previous statement (my view)? Hmm. Just by asking the question, you are agreeing that some conclusions are more right than others! You can see how any argument against this principle is self-contradicting and, therefore, invalid as soon as it is voiced.

We will address this style of thinking and its implications in the next chapter.

However, this brings up an important point in logical reasoning: there *are* right answers, and humans all agree on that point (not necessarily the answers themselves...just that there *are* answers!). As soon as someone stops agreeing with this basic principle, ask them if they think they're right or not.

This is called objectivity,[3] and it is good news. There is a right answer to the biggest questions that form our reality. In other words, there is actually a reality, a way things are, regardless of how I perceive them. Our task, then, is to establish a worldview that aligns with what is actually here.

There are several worldviews that attempt to answer the problems we perceive within human societies. Each view assumes a fundamentally different reality of how the world works, how it started, and many other fine details of life. Thus, like a chain, each view sets up a person for a certain outlook on death and the life experiences that result in suffering. Each worldview begs certain actions regarding how we relate to each other and the world (i.e. how we live our lives).

There are many more worldviews, of course, than shall be discussed in the following chapters. However, most people I have encountered find themselves within one or – perhaps even more troubling – several basic perceptions of reality. Does the chain of logical reasoning allow these worldviews to live together, and if so, what parts of them?

Some Objections

Before we start examining worldviews and how they shape our suffering, some objections might be raised.

An early objection might arise about this logic-driven approach and the word "faith", a common term in some worldviews. Faith is often inaccurately defined (both by people who hold a faith-based worldview and those who don't), as blindly believing in something that lacks evidence or reasons. Here is the definition that we will adopt for this book: faith is believing in the reasons a person has for what is true – even when that person feels otherwise, but lacks substantial reasons (other than feelings) to change their view.

Another objection could be raised in relation to my correlation of trauma and worldview. For example, if a correct worldview is so important for mitigating trauma, why do all people (across a variety of worldviews) still bear the wounds of trauma? Is it really the worldview that matters, or is it simply the depth of belief in the worldview that matters?

At first glance, we may be inclined to give more credence to this strain of thought than is due. Depth of belief matters – but only if that belief is true! Say, for example, that you didn't believe that people died. You might hold that conviction with unwavering belief – until someone close to you dies! Then you would be traumatized by that death because of your firmly held inaccurate belief! When reality hits, the foundation either stands or falls. "Denial," as Mark Twain says, "ain't just a river in Egypt."

Continuing to believe an obviously false principle is common among people, and it begs a question. Why?

Because it is hard for people to change how they live their lives. It is easier to go along and play the fool. Easier, that is, until hard reality shows up.

This may be why all cultures struggle with trauma. Most people don't actually know *why* they think the way they do. Thus, as I have already indicated, we can immediately start doing a favor for the people around us: hold them accountable to produce reasons for what they claim. The person making a claim is the one responsible for producing reasons explaining why the claim makes sense. Too often we let claims go unchallenged and unexplained, giving our brethren a pass. It is a pass into the dark folly of complacency.

You may think my approach sounds unreasonable. Perhaps, you don't want to argue with everyone about what they think, you smell conflict brewing. Shouldn't we just love one another and move on? Each person should figure out the truth for themselves, right?

Love (like faith) is one of those fundamental principles that people throw around without defining it. For now, consider this definition: love is doing what is best for another person, regardless of the cost to yourself, or the perceived worthiness of the recipient.

So, what is *best* for other people?

Here is my answer: to challenge them to hold a worldview that aligns with reality. Allowing a person to continue in falsehood, especially for years, may contribute to more harm than you think.

What We Learned in this Chapter:

The foundation of any worldview (or chain of reasoning) is *logic*. Logical reasoning has a certain formula that produces answers that fit together, like a chain, to explain what reality is and how reality works. Thus, like a chain, each worldview sets up a person for a certain outlook on hard life experiences and death.

This logical formula has three basic elements:
1. A claim
2. Reasons for the claim
3. An evaluation of those reasons based on their possibility, probability, and likelihood.

Reasons must not contradict other links in the chain, or the chain breaks and the worldview doesn't work.

We learned that a fool thinks both too much (they look for problems when none exist) and too little (they look for reasons that support their preconceived conclusion). Don't be a fool. Don't hesitate to think through problems and claims, even controversial ones.

We also addressed a basic concept in logic: there are right answers. This is called *objectivity* in philosophy and will be discussed in principle later on.

Lastly, we addressed a few objections that seem counter to logical reasoning. Faith and love are both powerful words that, when correctly defined, support a logical position.

Chapter Two Notes

---

[1] The basic reliability of sense perception is necessary to form any coherent conclusion about principles, abilities, or categories. Any counter argument is self-refuting, as it would consist of a perception. *"The Basic Reliability of Sense Perception"* by the C. S. Lewis Study Group is a concise article on this topic, worthy of further reading.

[2] The Law of Causality: There is no beginning or change of existence without a cause.

[3] A proposition may be considered to have *objectivity* when its truth conditions are met independent from individual subjectivity (thoughts, feelings, bias, etc.). A useful dialogue on the objectivity of knowledge, science, morality, ethics, and history may be found in the Scholarly Community Encyclopedia. Individual research on objectivity, as well as reading Plato, Descartes, Kant, and Newton, are good starting points.

Chapter Three

Power and Complacency: The Birth of Relativism

A popular line in the 2021 blockbuster movie, *Dune,* goes something like this: *"Life isn't a problem to be solved, but a reality to be experienced."*[1]

This is a claim, and it represents a worldview most often called relativism. Simply put, in this view there *isn't* a correct worldview – there isn't even a question at all. Everyone can believe whatever they want, build their life on whatever principles best suit them, and live and die as they see fit.

Now, this might appear convenient and simple right off the cuff, but we must not abandon reason. Does this claim logically work with *reality*? And if so, what implications must logically follow in this chain of reason?

I have encountered two distinct types of relativism. The first (and most common) is the cultural complacency birthed in the west through the separation of state control from personal freedoms.

In 1787, the Founding Fathers adopted the

Constitution of the United States. While the worldview of the Founding Fathers was largely uncontested,[2] they were explicitly silent on such things in the Constitution. As a majority group of federalists, the Founding Fathers did not hold that any particular worldview should be legislated at the national level. Secularism was formally adopted in 1789, when Congress enacted measures restricting the involvement of government in matters of personal freedoms, religion, and belief. This trend would continue into the 1900's, ultimately separating the government from upholding, supporting, or requiring any particular worldview.

This decision by the Founding Fathers had an involuntary side effect: a generational passdown of a certain style of thinking. During our natural stages of plasticity, people learn *how* to think, not just what to think. Western public schools are, at every level, considered an arm of the government. Therefore, each staff member and teacher is restricted in how and what they teach. Tolerance, impartiality, and equality are the keys to viewing the world as taught in western education – regardless of the inherent logical position or obvious falsehood of a given personal view.

From my experience as an administrator in public schools, the result is a stark avoidance from teaching, correcting, or even approaching any personally held view. Toleration of all worldviews and support of the freedom to believe *anything* has become a cornerstone of the western school environment and, by default, the adult graduates who now form our culture and raise children.

Thus, this form of relativism is natural in the West, due to the implicit separation of government from personal freedoms. As the government recedes from matters of speech and religion by mandating their agents, employees, and local units from suggesting a "right" answer, or even pointing out logical inconsistencies with obviously false answers, an implicit perception takes its place: there is no right answer. People (and especially children) are free to believe whatever they want, without any consideration as to what the consequences of these choices might presuppose in a traumatic event.

The western tagline "it is right for me" and "you do you" perhaps exemplify this worldview best. What appears problematic is how accidental the integration of this view is in the west. Acceptance of this relativistic cultural standpoint is practically required, unless you'd like to be stymied as a bigot, intolerant, or unaccepting.

In a word, relativism suggests that no view is uniquely right – everything is relative to the standpoint. Like all worldviews, the claim of relativism has several levels of complexity. Regardless of whether the worldview is accidental or unintentional, you know my rule: the person making the claim bears the burden of proving it. Relativism is a claim that, like a chain, builds and results in particular ways of living and processing trauma. Do the reasons for relativism make sense? Do they align with reality? A relativist must decide if the view can be held consistently, without inherent contradiction.

Universal, objective truth is the first hurdle for relativism. If there is no universal truth...wait. If there is no universal truth, is *that* a universal truth?

You can immediately see the problem. On the most basic level, relativism cannot be universally true without immediate self-contradiction.

Thus, there is actual truth. Relativism cannot logically be applied at this foundational level.

During the COVID-19 pandemic, my day-job was directing the risk, safety, and security functions for a mid-sized public school district in Washington State. During COVID, schools (as units of government) shut down as directives came in at the national, state, and local levels. Over time, those restrictions loosened. After about a year, the directives changed. The local health departments indicated that, when certain steps were taken, school was safe.

It was time to return.

This created more of a mess than we started with. I ended up at the bargaining table as staff forwarded the many concerns about their safety to administration. What was most challenging was separating opinions from fact.

As soon as we'd sit down (remotely) at the table, a barrage of concerns would come up, all centered around the risk of coming back and teaching children in-person. Most staff didn't want to do it.

"Who would you say is the most highly educated

person in terms of health, and zoonotic pathogens, and also bears the responsibility for the safety of citizens in our area?" I would ask.

The reply was quick and unanimous. "The local health authority and the chief health officer for the county, state, and nation."

"Right," I agreed. "And *they* are saying that it's not only safe to come back to in-person learning, it's necessary for the well-being of our kids."

The reply was immediate. "But *we* don't think it's safe! We need hazard pay if we're going to return."

"What else could we do to make our environment safer?" I would ask, thumbing through the thirty-page incident action plan I had developed for each school that spelled out the exact safety measures being implemented.

"There is nothing you can do to make it safe. That's the point!"

"But it seems the local experts agree that it *is* safe. What makes you think they are wrong?"

Round and round we'd go, for weeks. Months. Late into the night. We even brought in the chief medical officer for our county, who had reviewed and approved our plans, so staff could hear it from him directly. It did no good.

Where was the line between medical fact and public opinion?

As a secular institution, it seemed our staff had been trained to value opinions instead of evidence. The result was not pretty. Our school district went through three superintendents in quick succession and the operations team lost 80% of their leadership staff.

For reality to make sense, universal truth is a logical necessity. Some things are right, and some are wrong. As soon as a person disagrees, they find themselves in a contradiction...with themselves.

This might seem apparently obvious, so why then is relativism widely accepted? Right out of the gate, it seems to fall flat. From where does it stem? What chain in the anchor does it attach to?

There is another, less foundational and more controversial level of relativism.

Moral truth provides the next hurdle for this worldview. As we have already discovered, there is actual universal truth. Is morality one of those truths? Does good and evil actually exist, or are they fabrications?

As relativism has proven self-contradicting in regards to universal truth, it is upon the relativist to provide reasons to exclude morality from the assumption of the basic reliability of the senses. Morality appears real enough. So, what reasons exist for the relativist to claim they aren't?

I'm still waiting for a good, non-relative answer from a relativist on this question. However, we can examine what would happen to the links in our chain of reasoning further down the line if we assumed, for the sake of argument, that logical reasons to exclude morality from our 'truth basket' exist.

If morality *is* relative, it follows that good and evil are both illusions, based on nothing but the opinion and perspective of the people involved. Logically, a moral relativist must concede that evil does not exist. Thus, evil has never been done in the world. Likewise, good has never been done. There is no good – it is all relative. This view of moral relativism is a key principle in some Oriental worldviews, such as Hinduism and Buddhism.

Let's follow the chain of logical reasoning for moral relativism.

What happens when we assume morals are fabrications? What else, then, is a fabrication? Well, morality is the foundation for ethics. Ethics such as honesty, faithfulness, personal inalienable rights, freedom, and justice...these are all ethical conclusions based on morality.

To be consistent with our chain of reasoning, if good and evil do not exist, then ethics have no logical basis. In this view, there is no such thing as inalienable rights. Justice is not real, since no real wrong ever has occurred; it is a tagline, with no actual meaning. Honesty...come on, don't get me started! What matters is what you can get away with! And why be faithful? If a person isn't faithful to you, what are they doing wrong?

To be consistent in this view, it is impossible to do wrong. Wrong doesn't exist.

Of course, ethics are the foundation for laws. Genocide, rape, murder, molestation, enslavement, battery, assault – all laws founded upon ethical and moral considerations.

Without moral objectivity, none of these actions are inherently wrong. In fact, as long as a person gets away with it, toleration and equality dictate we should respect their different view; and maybe even offer benefits to such people to ensure they receive the same quality of life that others enjoy. Let's say a person enjoys beating women. Maybe that is natural for them. They identify as a woman-beater. Who's to say that's wrong? Sure, some others may not like that...but that is just their view. Nobody is actually wrong, just uncomfortable.

Very uncomfortable.

I run into uncomfortable people every once in a while.

Every year, my family writes a Christmas letter. While not always short, it highlights some of the adventures and lessons we have learned throughout the year. The idea is that, in twenty years, my children can see the trajectory of our life in a thirty-minute read. It is a way to include our loved ones, who live far away, in our daily life; and I use the opportunity to challenge each of them to live well.

One year, on the list of recipients was an old neighbor who, as far as I could tell, lived in a worldview where karma reigned supreme. Do a little good, and avoid a little bad. Do a little bad, do a little extra good. They were a neighbor and a friend. We sent them a letter.

That year, we had a use of force incident. It was a great story with many lessons, so I included a paragraph about it in the letter. Here's a part:

Dusk was falling. Maicie (4) proudly led the way, carrying the OC spray, as we walked up to put away the chickens. But what is this? Fresh, dripping paw-prints, as large as my boot on the concrete, put our head on a swivel! Each heart-beat foretold what would happen next: and out she came, the massive bear, from behind the car near the trash cans...

This bear had been around for a week or two, and we had tried every way you could think of to get it to leave. I didn't want to kill it, but when a 400lb creature threatens your family within a twenty-foot standoff distance, there is little choice left. I shot the bear in the head, killing it instantly.

Two years later, I was in court. Our old karma neighbors couldn't stand the killing of animals and sent our letter to the feds, along with an exasperated statement detailing how I was a domineering maniac who was illegally hunting on my property. It was quite a claim.

While we were waiting for the judge to arrive, the prosecutor and a few other attorneys in the room (there tends to be quite a few in a misdemeanor hearing session), were bantering around the front table. Apparently, they had all read my Christmas letter, and were continuing a previous conversation regarding their vastly different views on my life-lessons therein. I almost thought they would start wagering how things would turn out regarding my case.

I was relieved that all of the attorneys in the room came to my defense during this banter. All except the prosecutor, that is. And then the prosecutor said something horrifying. "It doesn't matter if he's innocent," she insisted. "Even if he didn't commit a crime, he has committed some other crime and deserves what's coming to him."

That was an astonishing claim. My mouth must have fallen open, because I leaned forward and a question sprang out. "Did I just hear you say that, in this case, you don't care if I'm innocent or not? Do you hold yourself to the same standard?"

One of the public defense attorneys (not my attorney, just another in the room) laid a hand on my shoulder. "Don't take this personally," he advised. "It's just how prosecutors are sometimes."

Wow. Fortunately, when the judge arrived, it took him about five minutes to read the letter. He looked at me and sighed. "For the record," he began, "I didn't write any of the laws that brought you here." Of course, we knew what he was actually saying. *This is ridiculous!* He glared at the prosecutor over his glasses. The case was dismissed.

What happens in relativism seems obvious. Those with the most power set the rules for human conduct. Even further, those in power set the rules for what is morally, ethically, and legally right. As power changes, so will the definition of right and wrong, based on the view of the people in charge.

Does that sound familiar?

Relativism has saturated western culture. Have you seriously considered its implications? On one hand, we must not force any particular worldview on others. Women can choose to kill their developing children if they perceive it to be best. Children can choose their gender if they don't like it. Any adult can put anything in their bodies that they like, and even take their own life – as long as it suits them. On the other hand, we scream for justice. We highlight historical and present evils. We long for the *good*. Laws are enacted and redacted. Presidents are elected and impeached. Nobody is wrong. Nobody is right. Or maybe, more accurately, everyone is wrong.

We can't keep our story straight.

How is that going to help us during real suffering? Does it seem *right*? We know relativism is a fact of culture, but is it a true reflection of moral and universal reality?

Let's look at the other side of the coin.

What happens when we assume good and evil actually exist? Honesty, faithfulness, personal inalienable rights, freedom, and justice are all real. These are fundamental principles that *measure* culture, every culture, to a Standard of right and wrong. They must, then, be transcendent of the cultures themselves, not obligatory to them. History is not defined by power, but by this external Standard of right and wrong. Some cultures have been closer to the Right, others farther away. Perhaps people's understanding of this Standard has grown, but the Standard has always existed.

Men and women are different, but both are endowed with the same inalienable worth. Freedom is a right, not a wish. Justice is a real reckoning, a measuring to the Standard that is written on the hearts of men and women across the world.

Laws, then, are only right when they are accurate reflections of the moral and ethical principles to which they answer. Laws can be unfair, biased, and unjust because there is such a thing as a Standard of behavior, a moral high ground. There are actual right choices and actual wrong ones.

This line of thinking leads us into a completely different worldview.

What is reality? What is the most possible, probable, and likely explanation for the way things are?

Let me ask you a simple, personal, yet precarious question. How must you live your life if one or the other is true? Can you actually live in accordance with the logical outcomes of your worldview? If so, could we reasonably anticipate how death and suffering might affect a person?

Moral Relativism

- Morality is not, like other universal truths and our senses, assumed to be accurate.
- There has never been a good or evil act in the world. It's just your opinion.
- You've never been wronged. It's just your opinion.
- You've never been right. It's just your opinion.
- Any disagreement or agreement you make isn't right. It's just your opinion.
- You don't have any rights - just opinions. Neither do others.
- You can choose to do and be anything you want...as long as you have the power to take it.

- Moral trauma is an individual's perspective, an illusion in terms of actual right and wrong. Guilt is a social fabrication.
- What you think about death is relative. It is all about perspective. It is not a question to be answered, just a reality that is coming.

Objective Morality

- Morality, like our other senses, is assumed to be basically reliable.
- Examples of real good and real atrocities make up the fabric of history and our own lives.
- There is a Standard of behavior that we all answer to, no matter what those in power or the majority think.
- You have done real wrong and real good. So have others.
- Trauma is real, a reckoning of reality and truth to experience.
- There are real answers to life and death.

Note that a morally relative worldview cannot mutually coincide with a worldview based on an external Standard of right and wrong. One view is right. One view is wrong.

In my experience, most – if not all – adherents of relativism don't understand the logical inconsistency with objective morality and relativism. So, they mix the two, by saying, for example, that anyone can believe whatever they like...*as long as* everyone gets along.

Notice the addition of objectivity into the relative view. This addition hasn't changed the claim. It has simply muddied the waters. The same principles apply. Only now, the relativist is applying a standard that transcends personal views.

To the worldview of a moral relativist, this is an impossible conclusion, a logical inconsistency. To the relativist, there isn't a standard. There isn't any higher ground. As soon as a morally right and wrong way of conduct is conceded, relativism has cornered itself into a logical contradiction.

Relativism, at the end, is an ideology of power. Whoever wields the most power sets the rules, whether anyone else agrees or not. If those in power value kindness, all well and good. If they don't, still all well and good. Nobody is wrong, because there *isn't* right and wrong. There are no answers, just perspective.

That's how relativism works.

I connect relativism and complacency because, in my experience, relativistic views seem to come up when it's easy. Sure, who cares what anybody really thinks…until we need answers. Sure, as long as we all get along there isn't anything truly right or wrong…until we are wronged. It's easy to 'agree to disagree'…until it's personal.

When evil occurs to you or those you love, was there a wrong committed? Is justice real, or an illusion? Is guilt a self-made or social fabrication, or our measurement against a real standard? Does that standard exist within us, or outside of us?

Relativism must stand in the ring against reality

and it will come to blows. Will reality knock out relativism, or will we realize there never was a contradiction? Are there answers? Or is life a journey to nowhere? And if so, what does that mean for how you and everyone else (including those you disagree with) are living their lives?

You can see how the worldview you hold changes everything. Logical thinking helps us find self-contradicting claims, while clarifying claims so they make sense. The answers we find must be compatible with all the other links in our chain of principles.

What We Learned in this Chapter:

Relativism is a worldview consistent with the absence of universal truth and moral truth. Therefore, in this view, there is no good or evil, injustice, or personal rights. It is all a matter of opinion.

Actions within relativism are based on power. Those in power set the rules of engagement. They determine what is kind and not kind, right and not right. When power changes, so does the definition. Thus, whomever has the most power dictates truth.

This claim appears to have several problems. First, it is incompatible with universal truth, contradicting itself immediately. A true relativist cannot disagree with a claim without clarifying that their opinion is simply their opinion – they aren't actually right about anything.

Second, relativism doesn't align with the reality we experience. Morality is real. Enslaving children for sex trafficking is a real evil. People really do have certain inalienable rights. You can be wronged by another, and they are truly deserving of justice.

Relativism forces us to take one of two stances on reality. Either there is a Moral Standard of behavior that is external to people and cultures, or each person and culture determines right and wrong for themselves, and none are more right or wrong than the next.

I related relativism to complacency because of how I most often encounter it. It covertly sneaks into other worldviews. It is a key intentional element in some oriental worldviews, such as Hinduism and Buddhism.

Chapter Three Notes

[1] *Dune*, Denis Villeneuve. Legendary Entertainment, Warner Bros, 2021.
[2] John Eidsmoe, *Christianity and the Constitution*. Grand Rapids: Baker, 1987, p. 43. Of the fifty-five Founding Fathers (delegates to the Constitutional Convention) there were 28 Episcopalians, 8 Presbyterians, 7 Congregationalists, 2 Lutherans, 2 Dutch Reformed, 2 Methodists, 2 Roman Catholics, 1 unknown, and 3 deists.

Chapter Four

Matter, Chance, and Science: Materialism

After his death in 2018, the family of world-renowned scientist Stephen Hawking, who's lifework was attempting to discover a 'scientific theory of everything', published a conclusion he never formally claimed in writing, but almost certainly agreed with: "The physical sciences can explain everything. Everything non-material is fiction."[1]

This is a claim, and it is the basis of a worldview most often called materialism.[2] I have encountered two distinct types of this view. The first is an account of origins, how the world and living creatures came into being; and the second, a view on scientific theory.

In 1931, Catholic Priest, mathematician, and cosmologist, Georges Lemaître, upended several traditional worldviews by suggesting that all existing matter began with the explosion of a single dense particle at a single point in time, which rapidly expanded into the known universe.[3] This "Big Bang" theory was corroborated in later years by Einstein,

Hubble, and many other notable names who concurred: the mathematics of relativity and the observations of astrophysics begged for a beginning, a single point in time when the physical universe began.

This historical account of the Big Bang theory does not surmise materialism as a worldview, however. Obviously, as a Catholic Priest, Lemaître held a particular view of reality and apparently could justify it with the conclusions he observed from the natural world. Materialism as a *view* is quite different from the application of the scientific method (which is, in short, a logical approach to analyzing the world). While materialists are renowned for touting the scientific method as their modus operandi, we must not confuse *science* (the methodology) with the modern view of materialism.

Materialism, as a view on origins, is a claim that everything that exists came into being through a derivative of matter and chance. Materialism expressed within scientific theory suggests that everything can be explained through matter and natural means.

The key view of both is simple: there is no external agent involved in the real world. Everything that happens, from the formation of galaxies to the decomposition of matter, is something that merely happens by chance. They aren't anyone's *doing*. They have no point. There is no purpose to any of it.

Obviously, this key distinction has not been held with many notable scientists in many fields, in both the past and present age. But, there is little doubt this view of random causation is the explicit assumption of materialism today.

Remember, the one making the claim bears the burden of proof. Does this claim logically work with *reality*? And if so, what implications must logically follow in the chain of reason? This chain will result in particular ways of living and processing trauma. Does this view of materialism make sense? A materialist must decide if the view can be held consistently without inherent contradiction.

In the beginning, there was a particle. *"An infinitesimally small singularity, a point of infinite denseness and heat."*[4] This apparently small point contained all of the energy for all of the expanse of the cosmos. Then, suddenly, it exploded.

We're only a few nano-seconds into this worldview and we have come up against our first set of logical problems for materialists. How can there be a beginning if there was already something physical there? For this to make sense, a static infinitude would need to be present as the foundational element of material reality. I am not a mathematician, but scientific research indicates that this is *not* what the math of relativity says.[5]

Even assuming a static infinitude of this primordial particle, how did it change to become anything other than its original state? It is a logical contradiction.

This logical impossibility stems from a key element of reality called the law of causality.[6] The law of causality is a requirement in mathematics, physics, cosmology, and every form of reality we know. Our observations of the universe, in our simplest and most complex forms, are derivatives of the law of causality.

The law is simple: there is no change of existence *without a cause*.

A ball does not roll on a perfectly flat plane without an exterior force. A vehicle cannot end up at the top of a hill, full of kinetic energy, without an equal or more powerful agent putting it there.

Materialism then, in terms of origin (and like relativism) falls flat right out of the gate. The story, as it's told, doesn't line up with reality. There is a page missing.

This was all a long time ago however, and (at least for me) it is hard to think of for extended periods of time. Materialism has other origins to explain that are closer to home. This worldview must also explain how this particular particle of energy came to form a key element of our reality: Life.

My father and I have had many robust conversations over the years. Mostly because our worldviews are so different. In my experience, his view has always been supported by a staunch materialism. I remember the first time I logically laid out the dilemma of origins for him. He paused, thinking, and then conceded, "Yes, I suppose some other sort of force must have stimulated the initial change at the Big Bang."

I wasn't about to leave this surprising concession

from my dad untouched, without pressing it to the next logical conclusion. The problem was, I never got the chance. Without any prompting, I received a well thought out materialist exposition of what happened *after*. The conundrum of beginnings was promptly side-stepped, and it swept us right into the views of what happened next.

The modern exegesis of 'what happened next' is relatively well known, as it is formally taught in every public school in the West. Matter cooled and condensed. The forces of gravity pulled particles together into supermassive balls which fueled other forces like fusion and electromagnetism, which then settled into equilibriums of varying sizes. Over a few billion years, things cooled further. Internal pressures erupted from volcanoes, spewing elemental vomit across desolation. It was a world devoid of oxygen, composed mostly of methane. And then, on the surface of earth, life appeared in its most basic form to kick off the cycle of evolution: microbes.[7]

Now, *that* is quite a claim.

Basic life consists of some complicated elements. The most basic form of life, microbial bacteria, contain DNA and RNA – the blueprints for life. At this basic level, DNA is contained in a chromosome, which rests in a structure called a nucleoid, which sits in the cytoplasm of a bacterial cell. Within that cytoplasm are fifty-five different proteins built upon structures called ribosomes, containing three types of RNA. Keep in mind, this is only for the most basic of microbes. Plants, for example, have an entirely different and more complex genome (in other words, a different type of DNA), though the size and complexity of DNA at this level apparently says little about the complexity of the organism.[8]

Bacterial chromosomes contain about fifty giant supercoiled loops of DNA.[9] The sequence of bases in the DNA has been determined for hundreds of bacteria. The amount of DNA in bacterial chromosomes ranges from 580,000 base pairs in Mycoplasma genitalium to 4,700,000 base pairs in E. coli to roughly 9,450,000 base pairs in Myxococcus xanthus.[10]

If any element within this internal structure fails to function properly, bacteria are unable to express their genes properly and die! This brief summary includes nothing regarding the complex external environmental factors necessary for the survival and reproduction of such organisms, nor the complex state of affairs necessary to capture and reprocess energy. Each is a required function for all living things.

According to materialists, every element of the above (and many more besides) randomly came together at the right time, in the right place, in the right order and became alive. The rest is evolutionary history.

It sounds like a nice bedtime story. But it is more than that, it is a claim and one that appears devoid of possibility, probability and likelihood. Life is here - that is an essential element of reality. How? Is this the most likely possibility?

Mathematicians suggest various odds of this all

occurring by chance, but most compare it to the equivalency of finding a fully functional 747 aircraft on an uninhabitable planet. As stated by a Stanford University publication, "When one is dealing with an accidental generalization, the probability that the regularity in question will occur gets closer and closer to zero, *without limit*, as the number of potential instances gets larger and larger, and that this is so regardless of how large one's evidence base is."

I read a defense of this conundrum by one materialist who countered by stating most DNA base pairs are made of only a few types of amino acids, thus making it more likely for this to all happen. Is it more likely for a plane to be found fully assembled because it's mostly all made out of metal?

While knowing the low speculative odds of this view is useful, it doesn't alleviate or expound the logical problem we have here. Even if you had all the right elements of life together – say, in a body – you don't get life. Add a jolt of electricity and…you still just have a body.

The law of causality rears its head again. A guitar has all the necessary elements to make music. A man has the necessary faculty to write a story. Many planks of wood form the necessary materials to make a house. In each case, something else must happen for anything to occur. In each case, an *agent* is required.

Have you ever seen a dead body? They often have all of the necessary components, the blueprints for life. But they are missing something, something we cannot give them, something beyond all the right pieces organized together.

They are missing *life*.

I have seen a few dead bodies. I remember one vividly. I was responding to a DOA call (dead on arrival). Upon arrival, the reporting party took me into a detached structure that looked like a mother-in-law residence. It was sparsely furnished, with a concrete floor and a few rugs.

There, on the rug, was a man who appeared to be sleeping. He was face-down, his head was turned away from me. He was fully dressed in shorts and a t-shirt. There was no blood. A magazine seemed to have slipped from under his left hand, and was lying beside him. It seemed certain that with a nudge, he would awake, take up his magazine, and be alive.

Then I walked to his other side.

His eyes were destroyed.

Now, to clarify, having eyes isn't a prerequisite for life. He was stiff though, in rigor mortis, which indicated to me he had been dead between one and six hours. As I waited for the coroner to arrive, I noticed something else. A dark band seemed to be moving across the floor. What could that be? I looked closer.

It was a colony of sugar ants, crawling across the ground as thick as a bicycle tube. Attracted by the amazingly high sugar content of this man's blood (according to the coroner, a likely result of his body trying to process the alcohol levels in his system), the ants had eaten into his eyes and were starting to work into his tattoos. I guess the tattoos somehow made it easier for them to get access to the sugars.

I never did hear from the coroner if the alcohol killed him or the sugar ants did.

Either way, our question remains: why wasn't he alive? He had all the necessary pieces! If I had put this body out in the primordial world, would it have become alive by itself?

Life poses the same problem as creation for the materialist. From where does it come?

When my dad sidestepped the issues of beginnings, he also sidestepped the beginnings of life. I find this often happens with materialists. They tend to skip right into how this view affects the rest of reality. It's a chain of reasoning dangling in mid-air.

This is a serious step forward that appears to lack logic. However, for the sake of argument let's pretend that we had reasonable answers to these two dilemmas. Where would the logical chain of reasoning of materialism take us? What would reality look like?

If everything is a byproduct of matter and chance, that means that every element of human existence is also a random byproduct that is devoid of purpose. Purpose cannot be derived from random chance, no matter how long or how intricate those chances become. In this view, there is no objectivity for the senses to perceive. Thus, human perspective is simply random manipulations of energy being output in a random array of information that has been guided, through evolution, into a beneficial form of adaptation.

Meaning is logically irrelevant from a random equation. In this view, morality, ethics, and laws are all occurrences that have evolved within the universe, historically helping us survive and reproduce. Outside of the human species ability to reproduce, moral elements mean nothing. Relativism can be taken to new levels: love is an illusion, a derivative of a chemical reaction and nothing more. Choice is a fraud that doesn't exist. Each person's decisions are merely their genetic byproduct and, therefore, they cannot be responsible for whatever 'good and bad' they do. Each person is simply evolving to their environment with whatever bag of genetic code they have been served by nature.

Good and bad are chemical reactions. Life is a random chance, ruled by the biggest bug, best adapted to survive. Death is the natural state of the universe. Agency does not exist at any level.

Human life then, as Hobbes famously termed it, looks "solitary, poor, nasty, brutish, and short."[11]

More complications seem to arise when we leave the human condition. If everything is random, then how can the objectivity, shown through mathematics, be true? Is this also fallible? How can infinitely recurring patterns exist from randomness? The basic assumption of the reliability of the senses, and even the law of causality must merely be a perception, an evolutionary byproduct. Whatever makes sense is just the right chemicals firing off in our brain – and they all got there by accident!

Logical reasoning appears to break down at this point, but we can deduce that materialism, when taken to its reasonable conclusion, means there is no purpose in anything. Even the goal of surviving as long as possible would presume that survival was good, but as both life and morality are conceived from a random state of affairs in materialism, both are devoid of purpose. Death and life hold the same inherent value: zero.

It seems strange, given this view, that any creature would be able to conceive of purpose at all. Would you be able to formulate an idea of light, if all you knew was darkness? As Hawkings aptly stated, in this view everything else is fiction. Yet even fictional stories are derived from a conception of reality. The best fictional stories are not accidental, they are derivatives of purpose.

I met a confused materialist one time in the desert of western Arizona. My family and I were on a road-trip, looking for cool rocks and lizards, off-road. Way off road, in fact. We were ten miles away from pavement, in the middle of BLM no-where. We hadn't seen another person in the area all day.

We punctured a tire. We had no service. No tow-truck was going to drive on the 'road' (more of a dry wash) we had traversed. Of course, I had the forethought to ensure we had a spare tire, ready to go for just such an occurrence. As I put the spare tire on, I noticed the lug nut holes were different. They were recessed into the hub. My socket wrench wouldn't fit. This meant my spare tire was being held by lug nuts that were only finger tight. I didn't have the right size tool.

It was nearing dusk. We began crawling back toward paved roads, hoping we weren't permanently damaging the car. Maybe if we put all the kids on one side of the car, we could make it with just three wheels. Fortunately, after about a mile, we saw a truck driving toward us! There was a full tool rack on the back! Unbelievable! So, we met Roger (who happened to be from the same little town my wife lived in for several years), in the middle of the desert.

Roger was a retired biologist studying lizard reproductivity. He had spent countless nights out under the stars and his heart was solid gold. He noticed how alive my kids are. Not only in their behavior, mind you, but their character is vibrant.

"You've done a good job with your kids," Roger noted. "It's important for them to know what's right."

Ha-ha! There it was! It was the claim I had been waiting for, while I had been slowly tightening the lugs. "What do you mean, Roger?" I asked.

He was happy to clarify by describing some of the many bad parents that existed 'these days'. As a side project to his biology, he had developed a website on the ethics that people ought to instill in their children. He showed it to me. "Teaching the right morals to our kids is so important," he emphasized. "They need to know what is right and wrong."

It wasn't long before Roger claimed he was a materialist, an atheist to be precise. He began struggling to keep his story straight.

"Roger, I'm a little confused," I ventured. "It seems that, on one hand, you're saying everything is random. Does that mean there is no absolute right and wrong? No real purpose, except one that we've fabricated in our minds? If yes, then why have you spent so much time caring about morality? And if you do think there is objective right and wrong, how does that make sense based on your worldview?"

At the end of our conversation he laughed, a big, warm laugh, and shook my hand. "Well, I guess I'm sort of a loose atheist after all. I'm going to think more about this, and I'm glad we ran into each other."

So was I. My wife gave him a hug, my kids gave him high-fives.

There are many other claims that I have encountered within the common materialist worldview. Claims such as macro and micro evolution, the development and use of language, and eliminative views of choice are examples. I neglect to discuss each of these claims - not because they should not be considered, but because each link in a chain must reasonably connect to the next. These links are much, much further down the line. Initial links set the stage for every other claim made within a worldview. If *these* links don't hold, none of the other links in the chain of reasoning have logical merit.

How much value does chance and luck have in your life? Have humans randomly evolved from bacteria? How must we live, and think about how others live, if this is true? What is the most possible, probable, and likely explanation for the way things are? How will this shape your suffering?

What We Learned in this Chapter:

In contrast with the scientific method, which is a mode of discovering reasons through consistent logical observation and study, materialism is a worldview based on spontaneous causation, random sequences of events, and unlikely probabilities producing a consistent reality.

While the adherents of this claim often tout the banner of the scientific method, this claim is rife with inherent contradictions and unreasonable assumptions. Two basic claims of materialism pose the same set of problems. The first claim is origins – the origin of matter and the origin of life. The second claim is regarding everything else about life – matter, morality, and the forces of the world.

In both cases, random causation provides an inadequate picture of reality. Similar to the claim of relativism, materialism is a worldview based on power, with a lack of objective morality, ethics, and purpose. The strongest survive and the weak perish.

In this view, death and suffering is simply the natural state of the universe.

Chapter Four Notes

---

[1] Hawking did directly claim, "We are each free to believe what we want, and it is my view that the simplest explanation is that there is no God...we each have this one lifetime to appreciate the grand design of the universe."

You can immediately see how this claim demonstrates a self-contradicting worldview (referencing relativism, atheism, and Agency (design) in the same breath). Whether or not the right worldview is equivalent with the simplest one is an unsubstantiated claim (one I am seriously surprised a theoretical physicist would make).

[2] According to the Merrium-Webster Dictionary, materialism is, "the theory that physical matter is the only or fundamental reality, and that all being and processes and phenomena can be explained as manifestations or results of matter."

[3] American Museum of Natural History, *Cosmic Horizons: Astronomy at the Cutting Edge*, 2000.

[4] Space.com, Publication July 26, 2023.

[5] The National Aeronautics and Space Administration (NASA), *A Hot Big Bang,* 2024. https://lambda.gsfc.nasa.gov/product/suborbit/POLAR/cmb.physics.wisc.edu/tutorial/bigbang.html

[6] The Law of Causality: There is no beginning or change of existence without a cause.

[7] Smithsonian National Museum of Natural History, *Early Life on Earth,* 2023.

[8] *The Cell: A Molecular Approach Edition 2*. The National Library of Medicine, 2024. This publication also states, "The genome size of many eukaryotes does not appear to be related to genetic complexity. For example, the genomes of salamanders and lilies contain more than ten times the amount of DNA that is in the human genome, yet these organisms are clearly not ten times more complex than humans."

You'll note this final thought is a claim that the authors produce no evidence to support. Is complexity based on the size of a creature? The number of body parts? Social structures? It seems clear the authors have never kept honey bees (see chapter 5).

[9] David P. Clark, Michelle R. McGehee, *Genes, Genomes, and DNA*. Molecular Biology (Third Edition), 2019.

[10] Encyclopedia Britannica, *https://www.britannica.com/science/bacteria/Genetic-content*

[11] Hobbes, *Leviathan or The Matter, Forme and Power of a Commonwealth Ecclesiasticall and Civil*. 1651.

Chapter Five

The Elements of Reality

Logical reasoning has apparently led us to dead ends. The most common worldviews in the west are rife with contradictions and implausibilities. Every day, we accidently and intentionally rely upon a view of reality that doesn't make sense. We tolerate outrageous claims and make some ourselves.

We tell our children they can be whoever they want to be, but then acknowledge they have certain inherent strengths and weaknesses. We claim that there is a purpose for our lives, and then don't bat an eye at materialism taught in western schools. We wonder at the stars, and then confidently assert exactly how old they are and how they got there. We wish people the best of luck, as if everything were a derivative of pure chance, and then assign blame when luck doesn't go our way. We give our condolences, but aren't exactly sure what that means.

I meet a variety of people in my Introduction to Lethal Force classes. All sorts of people: people who have been attacked, single moms, folks who want to exercise their second amendment rights, military and law enforcement, and more. I even get a few couples who think this class would make a great date (Surprise! It's not!). Many of these people stay after to share stories and ask questions.

One of the most interesting conversations I have had was with a self-described adult entertainer. She arrived on a Harley with a no-nonsense attitude and slick leathers. About half-way through the class, she showed me a feather she had found on the ground outside. "This is a sign," she whispered to me. "The Spirits gave me this sign. I'm supposed to be here."

This was quite revealing about her worldview. I wasn't going to disagree with her, yet. What she didn't know is that a key element of my Intro to Lethal Force classes is forcing uncomfortable questions about worldview (and their logical outcomes) on my participants. If you are going to carry a gun, you better be ready to face reality. You had better be choosing to live your life *well*.

When the class was over, she stuck around. I could tell she was bothered, and it didn't take long for the river to spill over. Within a few moments, I was facing a tirade of objections. "How do *you* think you can know what is right and wrong?" she asked. "Each person has to decide this for themselves."

Hmm. That was a claim. I asked her if I was wrong about anything I had said. She apparently didn't see the logical dilemma coming.

"You *are* wrong," she asserted. "Life just happens. There is no purpose. You just have to survive."

So…was she right about me being wrong, I wondered? I decided not to take this tack in our conversation. Her claims were divulging, and a logical club didn't seem like the most loving approach. However, simply letting her rest in an inaccurate worldview wouldn't have been loving either. I recalled her earlier statement about the feather – which she had clearly forgotten in the moment – and decided to remind her. "I know this is challenging," I offered. "But if you are *supposed* to be here, then it seems you were *supposed* to hear *this*. Why do you think that is?"

She gawked at me.

What elements of your reality don't fit together? We pretend that we have thought things through, that we've closely examined the chains of reasoning that ground our lives, when we haven't. The result is confusion and suffering. Trauma.

We *have* learned some valuable lessons in this investigation of reality.

First, we have discovered that there is universal truth. Without universal objectivity, the elements of reality simply don't work. The person who disagrees with universal truth immediately contradicts themselves by stating a truth – and assuming that truth exists. If universal objectivity is false, basic logical reasoning is impossible. Mathematics falls apart. If universal truth fails, reality fails.

Secondly, we have discovered that there is moral truth. The claim that moral truth is a universal law, a Standard, seems to logically align with the reasonable assumption of our senses. It comes as no surprise, then, that reality shows we humans have standards of conduct, which have existed cross-culturally and throughout history. As a rule, honesty is valued above lying. As a rule, faithfulness is valued above betrayal. As a rule, kindness is valued above disservice. As a rule, bravery is valued above cowardice. There are exceptions to these rules, but those exceptions seem to be consistently rare *exceptions* in human history, not the rules themselves.

The only available alternative to a universal Standard is that morality is mere opinion, dictated solely by instinct and electrical stimulus fired in your brain. Without an external Standard of behavior, good and evil are bound only by perspective and are complete fabrications. If this view is taken, the fallout is immense. If right and wrong don't exist, all legal and ethical values are also personal opinions, based on the power of those in control. Thus, it appears less likely that morality has changed over time, and more likely that our understanding of a Standard has been refined over time.

You can see that our first and second lesson in reality closely align. Our task, it seems, is to conceptualize which laws (both within the forces of the world and the human condition) are simple regularities versus relations between universals.

If the ground around moral truth sounds questionable, our third lesson in reality leaves little doubt as to its validity.

Our third lesson is that Agency is necessary for origins. The law of causality, a foundational element of reality, necessitates an Agent for creation. Either there is an Agent at work here, or the law of causality (and our basic understanding of reality) is inherently false. Only with an Agent is creation logically possible. With an Agent, there is no longer a logical improbability for life. With an Agent, having a Standard of morality, external to human perception, seems not only possible, but highly probable.

The pieces of reality fit together like a puzzle, waiting to be solved.

It seems we are left with little choice. Agency is a key element of reality. Yes, agency appears necessary for origins and is a likely prerequisite for life. This begs for further investigation. Some forces in the universe seem causal, that is to say they seem to be a mere byproduct of other effects. Yet other actions appear distinctive, as if unfolding from a particular view and heading to a particular destination. Some things seem devoid of purpose, while others seem ripe with purpose. Some things seem to merely happen, while other things seem done by something or someone – an Agent.

This exploration leads us toward our fourth lesson in reality. Implicit in this conversation, we have assumed that people also have agency, the ability to know the difference between right and wrong, take action, and invoke change. Of course, some things appear to merely happen with people. Have you ever sneezed at the wrong time, tripped on something silly, or missed a high-five? Sometimes, events seem to merely happen. Other times, *our* agency is clearly at work. We choose. Our choices can be good or evil, and directly affect others, nature, and the world. Of course, we should expect borderline cases, but the reason these borderline cases fascinate us, is because of how apparent our own agency is in other instances.

If we are going to accurately understand reality, we must first determine the difference between those actions that seem to merely happen, and those actions that are done by agency – the Agency of Origins, the agency of people, and any other external agency we have yet to logically identify.

Simply put, we have little need or desire to try and understand the goals and purposes of mere happenings. Mere happenings have no standards of success or failure. People (and any other agents) don't have any responsibility over or against things that just come about. If trauma is a mere happening, we may not be able to prevent it any more than a kidney stone.

As Lucco Ferrero says, "It would be both a category and a practical mistake to try avoiding a dog chasing you as if it were a flying ball, and vice versa. These differences become even more marked and significant when they bear on our relationship with fellow human beings (and with ourselves). This is because the explanation and assessment of, and interaction with the doings of human beings can be framed not just in purposive and teleological terms—that is, in terms of their goals or aims—but also, and much more importantly, in terms of such notions as 'reasons,' 'rationality,' 'justification,' 'responsibility,' and 'morality.'"[1]

Is a seagull accountable for pooping on a person? The seagull may well have reasons for pooping, and it may elicit a variety of responses from the person pooped on. But we know the seagull does not possess agency to the same degree as, say, a person. A *person* pooping on you is held to a different standard. A person is expected to have very good reasons for such an action, and is expected to articulate them upon demand. These reasons dictate obligations, such as if they *should* be pooping you, or *shouldn't* be and, therefore, *should* be held accountable for their actions and consequences.

In essence, *should* dictates accountability to a Moral Standard of conduct. It is a derivative of purpose. Thus, you, as an agent, have a purpose. You are also accountable to that purpose.

Just how far does agency go? I have been keeping honey bees for several years and I remain fascinated by their social behavior. Come fall, the honey bees (who are mostly female) drive all of the drones (the male bees) out of the hive. The drones that don't leave willingly are stung and dragged forcefully out of the hive, where they die.

Are the honey bees accountable for this violation of moral law?

You can see how this question depends on agency. My spouse, if she engaged in the same behavior with me (and then, for the sake of our example, other men over the next few years), would certainly be violating a moral law – even if she felt very strongly about the issue, or claimed it was natural for her. Are honey bees also an agent? Are they accountable for their actions, responsible for the choices they make? Or are their choices mere happenings that they can't change any more than we can change the positions of the stars?

When a bear breaks into my apiary, destroys my beehives and eats my honey, is the bear doing anything *wrong*? Isn't the bear simply doing what a bear does? On the other hand, if my neighbor Jacob breaks into my apiary, destroys my beehives, and eats my honey, we can all see: the issue has fundamentally changed. Jacob didn't merely do this because that's just what neighbors do. He chose to take this action, *knowing* that it was wrong.

Choice, knowledge, and power are necessary for agency. Without these three elements, there is no moral law to break.

So, it appears agency expressly ties into the Standard of morality. At this point, all we can claim is that agents – those things that have knowledge between right and wrong, choice, and power – seem accountable to a Standard.

I had a participant in my Intro to Lethal Force class who was mandated to take a firearms class by a court, due to a brandishing incident. He learned a lot about the law and using force, but it was my challenge to his worldview that shook him up.

He came up to me at the end and gave me a long, hard look.

"Is this..." he paused, thinking for the right word, "...a *ministry*?"

"Well," I responded, "I guess that depends on what you mean by ministry. If you mean that it's obvious Agency must be involved with reality and, therefore, our relation to this Agency matters...then yes, it is a ministry. If you mean I'm interested in producing some religious propaganda, then no. I am interested in you engaging your head and then, by necessity, your heart."

If we're going to make sense of trauma, this seems like the direction we must travel.

Defining agency against mere happenings is necessary at both a macro and micro level to understand reality. What is this Agent of Origins? Logic implies there are other agencies at work (such as ourselves). So, what implications do these other agents have on moral dilemmas and the after effects: i.e, trauma?

If we are to understand and come to terms with death and the hardest parts of the human condition, understanding agency is the key. Let's explore the consequences of agency in reality.

What We Learned in this Chapter:

Reality has at least four key elements. Any successful worldview must logically and consistently reflect at least these four outcomes:

First: there is universal truth.
Second: there is moral truth.
Third: there is Agency evident in origins, creation, and life.
Fourth: there is agency evident in human actions.

These four pieces of reality fit together like a puzzle, painting a picture of reality that aligns with our understanding of possibility, probability, and likelihood – all while avoiding self-contradiction.

The scope and involvement of agency in the world (and in our lives), is the key element to get an accurate picture of reality. Agency stands in sharp contrast to mere happenings, things that simply occur without any apparent responsibility or accountability to an external, Moral Standard.

This topic of agency raises further questions. It seems that knowledge, choice and power are necessary for agency, but there are clear differences between local agency (like people) and the Agency of Origins, the force that spurred creation and life. If we (people) are agents, there might be others.

Learning about agency is key to determining more about the reality of the world and contextualizing our experience of trauma.

Chapter Five Notes

[1] Luca Ferrero, *The Routledge Handbook of Philosophy of Agency*. London: Routledge, 2022.

Chapter Six

Local Agency

Agency is key to understanding reality and, therefore, our sufferings. So, who is an agent? We logically have determined there is an Agency of Origins. Are there other, local agents? What makes something an *agent*?

Some view agency as an element of emotional intelligence. In this view, feelings are causal of being an agent. Therefore, anything that experiences emotion has agency. Another view is that mere choice dictates local agency. In this view, the ability to choose between certain actions reflects agency. Other views suggest that social structures, self-awareness, or language determine agency. These complex structures infer accountability and, therefore, agency.

Each view, taken in isolation, comes across as problematic. It seems obvious that many creatures experience emotion, from pleasure to pain, and even more complex emotions such as despair.[1] Honey bees (an insect without a brain) seem to get angry, under the right conditions, and elicit many of the same behaviors seen in humans: posturing, escalating physical agitation, increased pitch and volume, and attack.

Animals also seem to display emotion. Dogs appear excited when their owners get ready to take them for a walk, or a ride in the car. Elephants display symptoms of joy upon meeting other elephants they recognize, but have not seen for a long time.[2] Are these creatures accountable to a standard of behavior simply because they feel? Is it right or wrong for bees to sting me when I am trying to treat them for a parasitic infection? Or is it a mere happening – is that simply how bees are, and there is no right or wrong about it?

Many creatures also display the ability to choose. Primates have been observed in choosing (or not choosing) to share food with another, when there seems little cause to do so. Almost all species of living creatures seem to have a criteria for choosing a mate, from spiders to fish to birds. A dog gives the impression of choosing to either obey or disobey a command given by its master.

Dolphins seem to be able to choose to intervene and provide protection, even for members of different species. Does this ability to choose make them responsible if they choose wrong? If a primate chooses *not* to share, is it wrong? If a dolphin has the capability to save another species and doesn't, are they violating some Standard of morality?

Complex social structures don't make our dilemma any better. I am convinced that honey bees have one of the most complex social structures on the planet. They have a governance system based on what appears to be both a monarchy and a republic. For example, when a hive reaches peak growth and is about to split, the hive will send out a few hundred scouts, within a radius of three miles, to determine suitable locations for a new home. How are these scout bees chosen from the rest? We don't know (neither do we know how bees are assigned their normal social roles).[3]

The bees cluster together outside of the hive in a large ball to await news. As the scout bees return, they report on the locations they have found with physical and verbal cues (which exceeds the definition of language), and pheromones. Eventually, some sort of decision is made. We aren't sure if it's a decree by the queen bee, or if a vote is taken based on the level of excitement regarding a particular location, but they all leave and go to the pre-viewed site and start a new hive. The process can take hours, or deliberations can stretch out over several days.

These little creatures don't possess a brain! There is no apparent disagreement, no stragglers that choose to stay behind. So, is this a mere happening? Is it even possible that a queen bee could choose a location that wasn't the best for the hive, simply because she thought it had a better view? Could a worker bee willingly stay behind in protest of the decision made by her sisters?

Perhaps you see the missing link. Regardless of complex emotional intelligence, social structure, or language, local agency appears dependent on two factors: the knowledge of when choices align to what *should* be (what is inherently right) *and* the ability to knowingly choose the wrong course of action.

Being a local agent requires the knowledge of a Standard between good and evil – what should and shouldn't be – and the power to choose between the two.

Therefore, the answer to agency in other creatures is logically obvious: we just don't know.[4] It seems possible, but not very likely in most cases. When a shark attacks a person, is it aware that it is a wrong action? Would the Standard of morality for a shark be the same standard in humans? While we can't be sure, there is one emotion that appears evident only in humans: guilt.[5] Only one species appears driven to redefine the bounds of natural law by force, from eliminating the consequences of reproduction to reversing aging.

You know who it is.

Humans.

While we can speculate on the agency of other creatures, we can be sure of only one case. Namely, our own. Humans have agency. We have a Standard of behavior. We have the power to supersede that Standard, the natural order of reality (what is *right*) through our actions...and we know it.

A few years ago, an old high-school friend of my wife was pregnant. They had discovered the baby would likely have a serious heart defect that would require heart surgery upon being born. My wife stumbled across a Facebook post from this distraught mother: "We have decided to spare our son future suffering by having an abortion. We have already consulted multiple opinions, so please respect our decision."

After I got over my initial shock, I couldn't help but wonder, is using lethal force a reasonable way to prevent future suffering? To be logically consistent in this view, who would we need to kill now in order to spare from suffering later? What about disabled toddlers? The elderly starting to suffer dementia?

How will this reasoning hold up when tested through years of pain and suffering?

It was her last sentence that was most telling. *Please respect our decision.* I knew exactly what that meant: *don't try to convince us. We've decided to do this.*

Something else seemed implied: *even if it's wrong.*

Her decision clarified something for me. We have a tendency to know when things are wrong, and we have the power to do them anyway. We rehearse our self-justifications, over and over, and they never quite seem to make the cut. They don't measure up to the Standard. It's why we keep reliving those actions (or in-actions).

That's how it's been for me. How about you?

As this standard of good and evil must have a source, it only seems reasonable that the Agency of Origins is responsible for creating this Standard of how things *should* be. Connecting the Agency of Origins and the Moral Standard is a logical step forward. Without it, we're left trying to fit in how a Moral Standard came into being without being created, when the logic indicates everything else *was* created.

This step further contextualizes this Agency of Origins, especially in relation to the only other agency we can be sure about (ourselves). If the Moral Standard was put in place by this initial Agent, then this Agency must be concerned with moral rightness among people. Moral rightness is both very broad and very personal – affecting everything from the governance of nations to the raising of children. Therefore, it seems reasonable to assume this Agent has a stake in both macro and micro levels of rightness.

A problem is now staring us in the face.

Humans, as local agents, are accountable to keep this Standard set by the Agency of Origins.

Do we?

What happens to a system when the components of the system choose to fail? It seems evident that the system breaks down. We aren't entirely sure how far-reaching the consequences of our failures, in this regard, go. Historical examples make it clear that even small actions, like how we interact with a single child in a single moment of time, can change the trajectory of entire nations and history.[6] A single negligent action by a single person in a lab can result in literal tears in the atmosphere of the globe.[7]

Therefore, it seems reasonable to conclude that even a small deviation from the Standard, results in an immeasurable fallout that likely builds exponenttially over generations.

So, when we look at traumatic events in the world — everything from the direct choices of people (to engage in 'wrong'), to the events of 'natural disasters' — who is at fault? How far-reaching *is* human agency?

It is apparent that our failings affect not only our own species, but others. To make matters worse, we seem to be able to negatively affect the fabric of natural systems, such as the water cycle and the weather. This is terrible news!

How have you infringed on this Standard and what have the consequences been? What have the consequences been for your children, and their children? How has our culture, in the present and in times past, broken this Standard of care? How has it affected the world?

> There is universal Truth.
> There is an Agency responsible for Origins and life.
> There is a Moral Standard, set by the Agency of Origins for humankind.
> Thus, the Agency of Origins has a stake in the rightness of human behavior.
> Humans have local agency, the ability to violate the Standard set by this Agency.
> Humans do and have violated the Standard. The effects of this breach are long-term, far-reaching, and serious at the micro and macro level.

Reality is starting to look a bit grim, but at least it makes sense.

Fortunately, the story doesn't end here. If it did, the future would look tremendously bleak indeed. We would be on our own, to get ourselves out of the mess we've made. To move forward, we must put into its proper place the only other Agency we know of, the Agency of Origins.

What We Learned in this Chapter:

Because the Moral Standard is an external measurement for local agents *and* it seems Agency is responsible for creation and life, it appears both likely and probable that this Agency is responsible for creating this Moral Standard of how things should be. As morality is a distinctly personal standard that affects everything – from how we talk to our children to how we govern nations – this Agency of Origins must be concerned with both macro and personal issues.

Local agency (in contrast to the Agency of Origins) is not a derivative of emotion (which many animals seem to display), or of mere choice (which also seems apparent in other creatures), or of merely power to change our environment. Agency is inferred when a creature has the knowledge of what *should* be (the Standard set by the Agency of Origins) and the ability to choose.

This knowledge requires self-awareness: the awareness of the Standard (what should and shouldn't be), and the power to choose between the two. Thus, while we can speculate on the agency of other creatures, we can only be sure that humans have agency. We have the ability to supersede the natural order of reality (what is *right*) through our actions...and we know it.

Therefore, humans as agents are accountable to keep this Standard set by the Agency of Origins. The problem is that we don't and we aren't sure how far-reaching the consequences of our failures go.

Historical examples make it clear that individual actions can change the trajectory of entire nations, history, and even natural laws. Therefore, even the smallest deviation of a person from the Standard, results in a fallout that likely expounds over generations.

So, when we look at traumatic events in the world and wonder who is at fault, it appears that we are a majority stakeholder in the preponderance of bad things that happen.

If we are going to heal, recover, and deal with suffering, we must not stop here.

Chapter Six Notes

[1] Oxford Academic, *BioScience*, Volume 50, Issue 10. October 2000, Pages 861–870,

[2] PBS, *Elephant Emotions*, October 11, 2010

[3] Honey bee social roles include queen attendants, nurse bees, guard bees, fanning bees, food storage bees, forage bees, and housekeeping bees...just to name a few.

[4] Oxford Academic, *BioScience*, Volume 50, Issue 10. October 2000, Pages 861–870,

[5] Jason Goldman, *Do Dogs Feel Guilt?* Scientific American, May 31, 2012.

[6] For example, Tim Berners can trace his invention of the world-wide web back to an electrical fix he made to a model train that his parents gave him. This single event turned his interest from trains into computer engineering.

[7] The National Aeronautics and Space Administration (NASA), OZone watch, https://ozonewatch.gsfc.nasa.gov/facts/hole_SH.html#:~:text=Chlorofluorocarbons%20and%20ozone,persist%20for%20years%2C%20even%20decades.

Chapter Seven

The Agency of Origins

At this point, many jump to conclusions. We don't like the idea of being at fault. Maybe it's this Agency of Origins that's really the culprit. If this Agency is all-powerful, as many understand it, doesn't fault belong there? Or, perhaps, this Agency of Origins isn't even around – the clock was wound, the rules set, and then it was a quick exit stage right. Maybe we are on our own.

From my experience, this confusion can often result in a rather spiritual outlook on life best summarized in the short phrase, "I'm not religious, but I am spiritual."

I've heard phrases like this a lot over the years. As best as I can tell, this most often means that a person knows there is more to reality than materialism or relativism would suggest, but is unwilling to commit to the logical implications of Agency and morality on personal life. While in strict philosophical terms, this view may fall into the realms of deism or pantheism (or many others), we will discuss this stance under the general umbrella of spirituality.

From my experience, spirituality is a view marked by Agency disengaged in current reality, Agency MIA (missing in action). This is a claim, and we must ask: what is the Agency of Origins really like?

We should start off with what we already know.

First, in one sense, the Agency of Origins must have an equal or greater amount of power than that which exists in all of creation. This is called the law of the conservation of energy, a basic principle of reality.[1] However, this power does not necessarily imply an ability to do *anything* (anything implies logical impossibilities).

For example, for other agents to exist, the Agent of Origins must allow local agents to take certain actions of their own choosing. If an agent can't choose, or doesn't have the power to affect change, there is no agent. And if an agent can't choose, there can be no Moral Standard – which we already know is inaccurate. Thus, when local agents choose, and especially if those actions bear far-reaching consequences, it logically implies that those choices can be counter to the desires of the original Agent. If the original Agent simply reversed those choices, eliminated their consequences, or made them impossible to begin with, local agency disappears. Generally speaking, this is called Free Will.[2]

Our experience of reality confirms a few other principles. Namely, that there are rules. I don't mean rules related to the Moral Standard, but rules for the general course of matter. Life and matter are, for the most part, consistent. When the temperature drops below thirty-two degrees Fahrenheit, water freezes. Consistently. Supermassive objects form gravity, which interacts with other mass. Consistently. In fact, we have an impression that the vast, intricate web of mass and nature operate under certain, consistent rules.

Does the Agency of Origins have the power to change these rules without self-contradiction?

Logically, we run into a dilemma very quickly. If the rules of nature changed on the mere whim of Agency, our senses wouldn't be reliable. In fact, nothing would be reliable. For all the ups and downs of life, life is for the most part consistent. If it wasn't so, would it be possible to derive consistent conclusions about anything? Imagine a world where gravity, heat, energy, and other forces were changed, even once. It seems unlikely that we could exist.

Let's apply this logical reasoning to a local analogy. We know that, as a matter of course, when playing Monopoly a person moves a piece around the board, earns resources, and uses those resources to buy properties. But what happens if those rules don't remain consistent? Let's say a person can take whatever resource they want whenever they feel like it. Do you see what happens?

The game ceases to exist. It just doesn't work.

C. S. Lewis uses the simple example of a piece of wood.[3] For wood to be wood, it must have certain properties: a certain density and tensile strength that allows it to support a tree, be made into chairs, be used for a house, made into a guitar, and used for fire.

Unfortunately, those properties also make it an effective tool for clubbing someone upside the head. If you remove the properties from wood that allow it to be an effective club, you also remove the properties that make it wood. It ceases to be wood.

Therefore, when implying limitless power to this Agent of Origins, we must concede that this Agent has orchestrated some cases in which power does not have as much bearing as we might first assume. Unlimited power doesn't help in these sorts of cases.

Local agency appears able to impact change, even negative change, to the order of the world set up by the Agency. Natural laws and occurrences must be regular and consistent for our world to be a world.

Thus, when a human – which contains a high concentration of water – doesn't bring adequate gear on an alpine hike and gets cold, they freeze. Sometimes, they freeze to death.

Is that a mere happening? Or is that a consequence of choice?

I met a young man late one fall whom I'll call, Kyle. He was from Kansas City, and had traveled to the great state of Washington for his best-friend's wedding. On the plane-ride out, he came across a YouTube video of the Three-Fingers Lookout: an abandoned fire lookout precariously perched atop the highest of three, 7,000 foot corresponding peaks, overlooking the treacherous Queest-alb glacier in the Cascade Mountains. The internet told Kyle it was a fifteen-mile round-trip hike. He figured he could beast that out in a twelve-hour day, up and back, no problem.

The internet didn't tell him that the river had washed out the road several years ago, eight miles before the trail head, and an even fresher washout moved that mark an additional three miles in. The total hike distance now? Thirty-seven miles.

I happen to know this trail relatively well. My son William and I summit a mountain every year, and we did this mountain for his 8th birthday (yes, he *is* a beast). Of course, we know the trail. We took the adventure bike through the washouts, cutting off that extra twenty-two miles. We picked late-August, when the crevasses in the glacier were wide open and the majority could be skirted around rock outcroppings. It was a glorious hike. We spent the night in the lookout, and the hikers we passed took bets on if William would be the youngest hiker to ever summit Everest.

Kyle had a different story.

Once he arrived at the washout, he figured he'd hoof it to the trail head. He made it, and then started up – six hours behind schedule. He hit snow at three thousand feet and began making less than a mile of progress every hour. Still, he couldn't bring himself to turn back. He trudged on, figuring he would make it to the lookout and overnight there.

He never made it.

My team found Kyle around two in the morning, at just over 5,000 feet, in twenty-degree crystalline temperatures and four feet of snow. Delirious from the onset of hypothermia, he had strayed from the trail and down a steep incline. He had the sense to crawl into a tree well, put on all of his clothes, and make an emergency 9-1-1 call.

Thankfully, since he was in the alpine flats, the call made it out.

He made it to the wedding.

It seems that water freezing is a natural law. It is a mere happening that is necessary for the world to work as it does. It also seems that a person chooses – either deliberately or negligently – to prepare for that reality. Humans, as agents, can (and, arguably, *should*) perceive that this is the order of the world, and take steps to avoid risk. This is why drunk drivers are held to a moral and ethical standard, as well as engineers when a bridge collapses. Captains are held liable when they sail into a hurricane. We *should* know the risk, and take steps to avoid disaster. Not doing so is a violation of the Standard and can have far reaching consequences.

The results of the risks we take are, once again, seemingly on us. Of course, we still take risks and often bear the negative consequences of them (or others bear the consequences). We choose to manipulate electricity in wooden houses, though we know it can cause fire. We choose to drive cars that go faster than humans are designed to go. We choose to use (and expose our children to) household materials that are known to cause irreversible damages, disorders, and long-term reproductive harm.[4] We choose to feel better now and take the easy road, knowing it will cost something in the future. Generationally these consequences build up, turning into maligned fortresses of past decisions.

We choose.

We suffer.

We experience trauma.

It almost appears hopeless.

But we have forgotten a key principle of our reality. Creation, the Moral Standard, and Life are all derivatives of Purpose.

Purpose.

As a local agent, we assume purpose. When we *should*, we immediately see purpose. When we look at reality, we see that this purpose is about what is right and good. It is not about being safe, avoiding risk, or living as long as possible.

It is about what is *good*.

Here, finally, we find the source of trauma. Deep in our hearts, we fear.

And what do we fear? We fear that our lives, our actions, or our inactions aren't or weren't *good*.

When your brother dies in your lap, bleeding to death in the field, what is it that you fear? When your child dies, when your parents wither away to dust, what is it that you fear? When we hesitate, when we cower, the same root assails us: we fear that it is not good. We fear that it won't be good, that there was or is no good purpose. We fear that it's not right.

Sometimes, of course, it *isn't* right. When a drunk driver smashes into a car, killing the occupants, it isn't right. Yes, we know this is our agency and the natural laws of the world at work, but...can't the

Agency of Origins do something about this?

Logically, it's hard to see how. It is unreasonable to assume there is any obligation for Agency to do so. We have no reason to assume this Agency owes us anything. These are our choices, and these are our consequences.

But *won't* the Agency of Origins do something about this?

We have reached a critical fork in the road of trauma. This question will define your worldview, and how you live through suffering. This question will determine the course of your life. There are only two possible answers.

Answer one: no.

Sure, you can be spiritual, but ultimately you are on your own, a ship without sails in an ocean of mere happenings.

Answer two: yes.

You are not alone. The Agent *is* involved in current reality. This Agency *can* and *does* draw near to us. This Agency *can* and *does* orchestrate events toward a good purpose.

You know my rule. The person making the claim bears the burden of proof. It is my turn to make a claim, and I stake my claim on answer number two.

An objection might be raised at this point by those who hold to a specific view, called the doctrine of providence.[5] This view claims that the Agency of

Origins has the power to orchestrate <u>all</u> events and actions, and does so for every single action both good and evil. In this view, the seagull pooping on your head was the result of the Agency's decision. A man's choice to come and assault your daughter would also be the Agency's will.

This view runs into dead-ends relatively quickly, as it eliminates human (and every other possible) agency. If every action is dictated by the Agency, then other agents don't exist. Thus, it also eliminates the moral law. How can there be a standard of behavior if there is no choice to follow it? Additionally, if this view is true, it eliminates all accountability and the course of justice. How can fault be levied against an agent who had no choice? It would be the same as condemning a tree as evil because it was cut down. Agents can't be held accountable when they haven't made a choice.

This view doesn't align with the totality of reality.

Is it possible that the Agency of Origins can orchestrate other agents' actions toward a good purpose, *without* exercising control over their every move (and, thus, eliminating their agency)? It seems obvious that it is possible, as we see it in our own experience. I can, as a good master, orchestrate the actions of my honey bees toward a particular destination that is better for them (and, non-coincidently, for me). As a good father, I often have an accurate view of how my children will respond to the choices before them. To a degree, I can even control *when* my children are exposed to certain events and choices. Thus, I can and do orchestrate their individual choices toward my desired purposes (hopefully these are good purposes, but this can work obtusely in the form of manipulation, fraud, or abuse).

If it is possible that I, in my human agency, can direct the actions of other agents toward a particular destination, it seems reasonable that the Agency of Origins does the same.[6] In fact, if Agency is personal and involved in our lives at the micro and macro level (as we have discovered from the Moral Standard), it stands to reason that this is *so that* our lives can be directed toward this Agency's good purpose.

A local analogy may be helpful, though the picture has many limitations. Imagine playing chess with a master chess player.[7] As is necessary for the game of chess, the players freely pick each individual move. However, each piece can only be moved in a few directions. Therefore, the master chess player can not only predict the moves of the other player, but can orchestrate the game so it ends up at the particular destination he desires – while allowing the other player to freely make each choice and, even occasionally allowing the other player to take back a move and try again.

Knowing that the Agency of Origins can and does orchestrate events, including my mistakes, toward a good purpose, has been key in my life.[8]

I remember a time when one of my family members was very sick. I was kneeling in my room, in the dark and quiet. I had come there to ask the

Agent of Origins a favor. I wanted the Agent to ignore the rules and heal my family.

As soon as I asked, I felt the Presence. It has been called by many names: the numinous, the mysterium tremendum, the fear of God.[9] The answer I received was clear and immediate: *Ask instead to see My good purpose within your suffering.*

This is not, of course, the first time I had drawn near to this Agency. The first time was the most traumatic experience in my life, because it shattered the inaccurate views I believed about the world and myself (that account is written in a separate book, *Forged Through Fire*). My direct experience (and the experience of many) implies only one of two logical possibilities. Either everyone who agrees with this worldview is completely nuts, or this logical equation takes us all the way to the feet of an Agency who chooses to be personal with us.

In fact, my whole life seems to revolve around a single, good purpose: drawing nearer to this Agency. I've had to be knocked down, drug about, and coaxed in – most often because I desperately cling to worldviews that don't make any sense.

Sometimes, when I play Monopoly with my kids, they make a stupid mistake and I let them take it back. Or I change my next move, knowing that my purpose for *them* is good, even if it costs me. I can do this without changing the rules of the game, because of my agency, my knowledge, and because I love them. It's personal.

My experience indicates that the Agency of Origins draws near and works toward a good purpose for us, even if it costs Him dearly.

Our worldview is getting specific and additional objections might be raised.

First, and perhaps most importantly, what if you don't have direct experience with this Agency? Even harder, what if you have sought this Agency out in a time of need and the answer wasn't what you expected or wanted?

My father once told me his catalyst for walking away from Agency in the world. From what I recall, he was a young man and loved his sister. His sister was in a serious collision. She was in the hospital, dying. My dad asked the Agency of Origins to intervene and cause her to live. She died.

This experience stands in stark contrast to my own, but it is certainly a shared experience. Some people find this Agency active and present, and others seem to find dead air. How do we justify this difference?

In the cases where Agency appears absent, there are only a few possibilities that could align with our current reality chain: either this Agency is MIA, or this Agency is preferential (absent to some and not others), or this Agency is not willing (or able) to give what is asked because it isn't best.

We learned in chapter one that trauma is the result of a failed test, reality vs experience. Our reality in these difficult times must be accurate to avoid trauma.

The first case, Agency MIA, seems impossible.

There is no explanation for Agency being apparent in my own story and countless others, except for the fact that Agency is personal and present at some level.

The second case, a biased Agency, raises thoughts of mystical rites that must be correctly performed in order to be granted an audience, or a certain kind of person who has earned the ear of Agency, or an Agency that dwells in a particular place that must be accessed through a particular means (a sort of real-life magical cave of Ali Baba).[10] This line of thinking quickly breaks down. It only takes one murderer to be heard by this Agency to demonstrate that this has nothing to do with a certain kind of "good person" (see slave-trader John Newton's (1772) story for a good example). Similarly, this Agency seems evident in a vast number of different spaces, places, and times, with no apparent consistent formula for "summoning".

In each case, it comes across like we're treating the Agent of Origins like a circus monkey, rather than the author of everything, the final justice of the Standard, a King. This Agent appears both near and far, almost like how we perceive the stars. Dare we restrict this Agent to particular rites or places? Can we bend this Agent to our own will?

It seems obvious the answer is no.

This leaves the third option. As already has been demonstrated, there are clear cases where this Agency does not appear able to intervene due to impossibility or logical contradiction. Nonetheless, like in Monopoly with my kids, we can't help feeling like there are occasional exceptions, where this

Agency is willing to break the 'rules' because of how personal He is. By definition this would be called a miracle, and implies a rare occurrence (the rules can't change permanently without changing reality). Why and when the Agent of Origins chooses to break the fabric of law set by His own hand, can we ever know?

However, I think we can logically conclude that this rare intervention has nothing to do with quid pro quo. What can you give this Agent that isn't already in His possession or ability to create? And what can you take away? The law of the conservation of energy makes this pretty clear. Nothing. This Agent is above any manipulation. When this Agent acts, the only option left is that He acts simply within His good purpose.

So, is there a good purpose that is greater than avoiding death?

This, of course, depends on how you think death fits into reality. Is it an ultimate ending, like materialism suggests? Or is it where local agencies lose all identity of self and merge with the Agency, as reflected in many cases of spirituality? Or is it merely the end of one chapter, that leads into another?

It may seem like we can't know, but why not apply some basic logic to the question? The law of the conservation of energy indicates that nothing is ever fully removed from the system. That undermines the materialistic view. The spiritualism view doesn't serve us any better. The destruction of our self-awareness and the absorption of all we are into the infinity of the Agency seems to immediately negate any value of the person in question. If that is reality, then what is the point of having a Moral Standard in the first place? In this view, does how we live our life matter? It seems like it wouldn't.

We are left, then, with the view that there is *something* on the other side of that dark water we call death. If so, then it stands to reason that avoiding death may not be as important as we make it out to be. This becomes obvious when we realize that everyone dies. It is a universal condition, a mere happening. Escaping death, then, is impossible! When put this way, it does not seem surprising that everyone dies, even when we ask the Agent of Origins to make an exception.

Perhaps changing the rules to avoid death isn't best after all.

Perhaps dying *well* – by living well – is much more important. What we know is that our actions in the present *matter*, and they seem to matter a lot.

What We Learned in this Chapter:

It seems we are a majority stakeholder in the 'at-fault' department. The consequences of our failures (both deliberate and negligent) are unknowable, but appear exceptionally far reaching – crossing over into even the basic forces of nature set into motion by the Agency of Origins. To make sense of this reality, we will have to discover a few basic facts about the Agency of Origins.

First, in one sense, the Agency of Origins must have an equal or greater amount of power than that which exists in all of creation. However, that power does not necessarily indicate the ability to do anything, as *anything* implies logical impossibilities.

Second, we find that the Agency of Origins has set specific ways creation interacts. These rules are necessary for the world to exist, and can't be consistently changed without destroying the fabric of reality. People, as local agents, are generally aware of these rules and break them anyway. When things go wrong, we fear that we have landed outside of what is good.

Thus, we mutually find the bedrock of trauma and its logical conclusion. Trauma stems from a fear that an action or experience is not good, not right. If the Agency of Origins is MIA, as is the case in spirituality, then trauma leads us to a hard dead end.

But there is another option, dictated by a logical derivative of purpose: Agency intervenes for our good.

We discussed the doctrine of providence and the actions of Agency. We learned that providence (Agency unilaterally directing all decisions and actions) without personal agency is a logical impossibility, as it negates the Moral Standard and, therefore, any personal accountability for that Standard.

We also addressed a possible objection, namely the lack of direct experience with the Agency in difficult times. It becomes apparent that this Agency is not a tool we can manipulate to our own ends. This Agency's actions are good and move toward a purpose. Thus, it follows that there is something on the other side of death. Therefore, actions in life matter considerably more than escaping death. This is logically compounded by the fact that everyone dies. It is a universal condition.

Living well (and, by connection, dying well) must be more important than the impossibility of avoiding death.

Chapter Seven Notes

---

[1] The law of conservation of energy states that energy can neither be created nor destroyed, only converted from one form of energy to another.

[2] Free Will is defined by Merrium-Webster as, "freedom of humans to make choices that are not determined by prior causes or by divine intervention."

[3] C. S. Lewis, *The Problem of Pain*. New York: Macmillian, 1944.

[4] While this could be referencing many of our regular household items, drugs, and supplies, I am directly referencing plastics. The material we make Legos out of. If plastics can have this level of impact, what else are we responsible for? Reference the National Library of Medicine for further information.

Amran, Nur Hanisah et al. *"Exposure to Microplastics during Early Developmental Stage: Review of Current Evidence."* Toxics vol. 10. Oct. 2022.

[5] The classical view of the Doctrine of Providence holds that every event — including human thoughts, choices, and actions — occurs according to God's will.

[6] Thomas Aquinas shares a useful analogy. Our mistakes, he says, are like limping, in which the defective motion arises from the crookedness of the limb, rather than the power of locomotion that impels it.

Thomas Aquinas, *Summa Theologica* I-II, Q. 79, Art 2.

[7] C. S. Lewis, *Miracles*. London: G. Bless, 1947.

[8] It may be helpful to think of another analogy (remember, every analogy has its limitations), of an author writing a story. In this case, the author exists outside of time (and the individual decisions made by characters) in the story, yet the author knows the decisions of each character and directs them toward a good purpose.

[9] Rudolph Otto, *The Idea of the Holy*. London: Humphrey Milford Oxford University Press, 1926.

[10] Edward William Lane, *One Thousand and One Nights*. London: Chatto and Widus, 1882.

Chapter Eight

A Context for Trauma

Reality, it seems, leads us to a particular destination. Logical reasoning sweeps us toward undeniable conclusions. Our worldview, as a chain, requires particular links to fit with reality:

One: there is universal Truth.
Two: this truth – along with all Standards of behavior and rules of nature – have been set by an Agent, the same Agent of Creation and Life.
Three: this Agent has a Purpose that, according to the reflection of the Moral Standard, is Good. We, as local agents accountable to that Standard, are a part of that Purpose.
Four: we *can* and *do* choose to deviate from that Good Purpose. The effects are devastating.
Five: Our deviation does not impede the Purpose of the Agency, because the Agency is personal, shown by the personal nature of the Moral Standard and the direct experience of humans. The Agency chooses to draw near to us even at

great cost, and orchestrates events toward a Good Purpose.

Six: Death, as a rule, appears to be a mere happening that can't be avoided and logically is not the ultimate end. Therefore, it looks like the Agency is more interested in us living *well* than avoiding death.

Neutrality regarding these elements of reality simply isn't possible. Our reasons and outlook on these core principles define how we live, what we think is important, where we think we came from, and how we suffer and die. Note how I indicate that it is our reasons, not the level of belief we have for these issues, that define our life. Beliefs without good reasons die, and they often die hard. Reasons that make sense last.

Avoiding reasons is impossible when suffering comes.

Finding answers that make sense with reality is the only way.

It is possible (and, arguably, likely) that answers to these fundamental questions about reality have been around for a long time. Allow me to recount a very old story.

In the beginning, God created the heavens and the earth: the forces, the elements. Everything you see, and everything you don't see. And it was good. God said, "Let there be life." And there was, teaming life of all kinds and forms.

Then God said, "Let us make man and woman in our own image, an agency reflecting our own nature. I shall make them responsible." He did, and He blessed them.

And it was very good. The Standard, the purpose: both were very good.

Thus, the heavens and the earth were made and man given agency.

It would not last.

God and mankind were not alone. Another agent was there: the accuser. The enemy.

"Can you really trust God's plan?" he whispered. "Is this really good? How can you be like God, unless you know wrong?"

So mankind made a choice. They took matters into their own hands, exercised their agency.

They turned away from God.

They ate of the knowledge of good and evil. They saw. And they became afraid, afraid that what they had done was not good. A new reality became apparent to them: evil.

Their fear was justified. The ground was cursed. Their choice affected everything, the very fabric of creation. They hid.

But God did not abandon them. He came for them, clothed them to ease their distress, comforted them.

Even so, the consequences could not be undone. Brokenness. Trauma. Death.

"My son, my beloved daughter," He called. "What have you done?"

This is a brief recount of Genesis 1-4, an account written 3,500 years ago.[1] The rest of this old narrative is about God's purpose, a King's purpose, to reclaim what had been lost by man's agency through an intervention of His own. A miracle. Yet, one that retained the integrity of the Laws He had created from the beginning. For the real God cannot contradict Himself.

It sounds like a nice story. It is more than that, it is a reflection of reality, a comprehensive reality. Any other context for trauma doesn't have real answers.

It is time for some answers.

The most important context to remember before, after, and through trauma is that God has a good purpose. He can, does, and will work out that purpose for your good. Do you remember Vincent from Chapter one? Remember that Dave used his agency and talked him out of committing suicide? Well, Dave and I didn't know we were both involved in that incident until twelve years later, three months after he had begun work with the TTA. We were teaching a corporate group in La Grande, Oregon, when Dave shared his story. He had no idea I had been right behind Joe.

More than a decade after the fact, we were sharing that story together to help others face their suffering. Coincidence? A mere happening? I was standing in the back of the room, as white as a sheet, not because I was afraid or re-traumatized – I was overwhelmed at God's purpose. He had continued to work through this horrible event for my good.

Remember Austin? You know, the guy who leaned on Satan's agency to help direct his decisions to come kill my family? While I was applying first aid, my son (six) was watching from the top of the stairs. "Austin, if your son was watching you bleed to death, what would you say to him?" I asked.

Austin turned his head toward my son and made eye contact. He was silent for a moment. "Fear God, boy. Because if you run like I have, you'll never run far enough."

I will never forget that. Neither will my son. "Austin," I whispered. "You must believe that God still has a good purpose for your life. You must choose what is right, even if it is hard...it can be *good*. You can be a part of that good. You are, today. Though you had intention of evil, my God has planned it for our good."

Remember that blown tire in the desert? That was my fault. I should have let the air out of the tires, but I didn't want to take the time to stop. I knew it beforehand, and I kicked myself for it afterward. But God had a good purpose, even with my lazy negligence: Roger.

Remember Kyle? Twelve hours later, that mountain had two additional feet of snow. As it was, in the clear night we were able to follow his tracks, seeing when he left the trail. Even with thermals, we wouldn't have spotted him in the treewell without those tracks. A half-mile lower on the trail, and there is no cell service. A half a mile farther up, the trail crosses Tin Pan Gap and enters the glacier, where even a small tumble would have dead-ended (literally) in a crevasse. If any circumstance had changed, he would have died.

"Kyle," I reminded him on the way down, "in case you haven't put the pieces together, you must still have a purpose here. Don't forget."

I could go on and on and on. My life is filled with mistakes! Mistakes of my own doing, mistakes of others, and the mistakes of our forefathers that I will never fully comprehend. In the midst of it all, there is God's unmistakable purpose.

It is for my good.

God has a good purpose for you. He loves you. Yes, even now. Remember our definition of love: *doing what is best for another regardless of the cost or the worthiness of the recipient.*

Instead of working from the ancient texts of the Biblical story outward, we have followed reality inward and discovered that, so far, that story aligns with the truth. This is a real context for trauma. We must know that this Agent of Origins is a King, holy, cardinal, acting, caring, and involved. He can orchestrate events for our good even under the crushing weight of our (and others) natural consequences.

When I wake up in the morning, I don't tell myself that it will be an easy day. It may not be. It might be the day my choices (and others) catch up to me. Lying to ourselves about reality won't get us anywhere. I *can* tell myself that God has a good purpose for today, and He will bring it about. I can walk in this broken world, knowing where my allegiance lies.

When my children get sick, I can remind myself

that there is a good purpose that supersedes death. When I and my loved ones are attacked, I can remind myself that there is real agency at work. I can remember that, even in the midst of great evil, God *can* and *does* work His purpose for my good. When I stand before a grave, I can recall that it is not the end. There is a purpose that endures.

Having faith in God's plan (remember the definition of faith? Believing the reasons you have for what is true, even when you might feel otherwise) is the sole source of healing, perseverance, and hope within dark times. All that is left for us, then, is to simply submit to this plan, and choose to do the next right thing, one thing at a time, until we have fully surrendered to His purpose.[2] Faith turns into allegiance, a life of dedication to and dependance on this King and this purpose.

Our agency does not disappear. Our consequences do not disappear.

Trauma does disappear. We begin to see that all things can be worked together for our good. Life just begins to look, well, *right*.

What comes next?

Well, then comes victory. Victory, in fact, becomes guaranteed.

What We Learned in this Chapter:

In this chapter, we learned that there are six linked elements of reality that lead us to a particular destination:

One: there is universal Truth.

Two: this truth – along with all Standards of behavior and rules of nature – have been set by an Agent, the same Agent of Creation and Life.

Three: this Agent has a Purpose that, according to the reflection of the Moral Standard, is Good. We, as local agents accountable to that Standard, are a part of that Purpose.

Four: we *can* and *do* choose to deviate from that Good Purpose. The effects are devastating.

Five: Our deviation does not impede the Purpose of the Agency, because the Agency is personal, shown by the personal nature of the Moral Standard and the direct experience of humans. The Agency chooses to draw near to us even at great cost, and orchestrates events toward a Good Purpose.

Six: Death, as a rule, appears to be a mere happening that can't be avoided and logically is not the ultimate end. Therefore, it looks like the Agency is more interested in us living *well* than avoiding death.

This reality stands in stark contrast to many who counsel the traumatized. Rabbi Kushner in his book, *Why Do Bad Things Happen to Good People*, suggests that bad events happen by mere chance, and

God does not have a purpose He can orchestrate through these events. Jerry Bridges in his book *Trusting God* suggests that God is in complete control of everything, even the actions of those making evil decisions, and that nothing happens against His will. Bessel Van Der Kolk in his book *The Body Keeps The Score* indicates that medication to correct chemical imbalances in the brain is powerful, but not anywhere near an end-all solution – every person must choose their own path of right and wrong, and explore it to its ultimate destination.

While each of these perspectives are insightful, they can't keep their story straight. They don't align with the full reality.

Instead, our destination appears to align with the story of Genesis, nothing added, nothing redacted. This story, God's story, reflects a picture of reality (how things are). Instead of a self-help dogma in the face of hardship, we need a real Agency, a real Helper, a real King working for our good even in the midst of the evil we create and suffer from.

When we look closely, that is exactly what we find reflected in Genesis.

God has a good purpose for our lives. This is our sole context for present trauma, and preventing future trauma. God loves us, according to the real definition of love. Having faith in that (according to a better definition of faith), is necessary during dark times.

What comes next is a choice: to pledge allegiance to this King and submit to His plan, or to resist and go out on our own.

When we ally ourselves with the King, victory is guaranteed.

Chapter Seven Notes

---

[1] David Rohl, *A Test of Time*. London: Century Ltd, 1995.
[2] S. R Harris, *Ella's Journey*. Seattle: Pacific Book Publishing, 2023. A highly recommended children's book to illustrate this concept within pain and suffering.

Chapter Nine

Victory Guaranteed

Let reason kneel outside in reverence, while love and faith enter further in.[1] Tozer's advice is hard for me to hear, but we must not forget that it is God who has given us both love and reason. Reason has taken us this far, but it is love that must draw us further in. To know is merely to lack ignorance. To love is to commit. To commit is to change.

I find love harder to write about than reason. Logical thought flows from one link to the next. But love? Love seems to be the more perilous of the two. When you first fell in love – with anything – did you know it was happening at first? Was it logic that drove you? What's funny is that we have a tendency to logic ourselves into our loves, not vice versa. We tell ourselves what we want to hear, not the objective truth, when our hearts are already committed.

At first, your love was probably just an interest. You felt inclined to draw near, but didn't have much context. So, you began to seek out this interest. As you spent more time near it, you sought to understand it, and began to understand more about yourself.

This, of course, makes good logical sense. We can't know ourselves without context. That critical context sharpens the lines of our existence. Some loves stop there. I have found that love can take another, deeper step, when it puts you into the *correct* context. In the end, love humbles, and in that lowly place it reaches its greatest height. Love, in this place, is both a terror and a comfort. A terror because you realize that what you once played with is entirely beyond you: beyond control, beyond influence, even beyond reason. Yet, it is a comfort because it is the closest you have ever come to being fully alive. It is the closest you have ever come to seeing God.

It was at that moment you became committed.

I think most people would agree that this process is not dependent on logical reasoning, and I would hypothesize that this is why so many people start strong and then die on this patch of 'love' ground. Love without reason tends to betray us. Not only does love have a tendency to initially blind reason, it also can affect a strange permanence to whatever is related to it.

Love is a carrier, if you will, of ideals. Our hearts flicker, and then we set out building shrines. We often mistake a lesser for the Greater, and end up idolizing a fraud: the beauty of woman, the strength of man, the inexhaustible depths of a baby's eyes, the vigor of youth, the crystalline fractals upon the alpine heights, the exhilaration of discovery, the electricity of a caressing touch. In each case, there is an echo of eternity, a taste of the Agency of Origins, a taste of Kingly Love. In each there is a reflection of power and knowledge, beauty and fullness, life and holiness. We are humbled, and we can practically reach out and touch that *very good* spoken of in Genesis.

Without reason, very good can become the shrine housing the worst sort of very bad. The vigor of youth can be sought after above all else, enslaving the person to a vision of the past, at the expense and detriment of self and others. A mother's love can become enslaving for both child and adult, confining under a stifling blanket of control and manipulation, instead of providing agency. A commitment toward God can change into a book of rules, checkboxes to reach a state of enlightenment; or avoid punishment. Even the love for self can enslave: the need to be seen as valuable, changing how you hear compliments and criticism necessary for life.

As these shrines get bigger and more entrenched within our lives, the farther away the *very good* of reality seeps. Yet, we never can quite avoid the truth. When trauma comes, these shrines are shaken. Sometimes, they are destroyed. We reach out for them and our hand passes through thin air. What we thought was real, what we loved, turns out to be a shade, the ghost of an idea.

This is trauma.

If we can screw our heads back on, we will discover the reason: we have supplanted the source of our love with the object. We have fallen for a reflection instead of the real. Our reason helps us to value the real experience without crowning that experience as King. Love allows us to enter in, but it is our reasons that provide the bedrock love must rest upon, to align with the good purpose of God.

For victory to be guaranteed, we must have a firm foundation. We must see ourselves and the world rightly. Then (in reverse order or simultaneously) we must learn to love the Source. In whichever order these two events occur, only with both of them will we see everything in the right context. Reason and love support each other to create a bond of fidelity.

Together, they draw us into His good purpose and keep us there.

This brings victory.

Thus, loving God (or anything, for that matter) requires us to see ourselves rightly. You might think you love your partner or your kids, but until you actually see yourself in contrast to their sacrifices, joys, and sorrows, you will never truly know love.

So, who are you? What do you bring to the table in this relationship?

Unlike lust, the first picture we get of ourselves from real love isn't pretty.

Let us return to reason for a moment. God has built a particular world, with consistent rules. Water freezes. People have agency. We are accountable to a Standard. We know that when we break this Standard, what follows are consequences. Those consequences appear to be bad – both locally and far-reaching.

In the end, it becomes clear that the Master chess

player played the board perfectly. If God has a good purpose and there is an end, it seems that end will be good. Therefore, it stands to reason that within God's plan, wrongs must be righted. Mistakes must be put right, and we all know righting wrongs takes more effort than making them.

Therefore, wrongdoing necessitates a reckoning. Justice is one of God's fundamental laws. He is a King, after all. This reality must happen, but it puts us in a predicament. Can we pay the cost of our immorality? Can we right the countless layers of error we have embedded in the world and ourselves?

The culture of the west appears saturated with self-help recipes, and they all feel reminiscent of a 'me-first' montage: *tell yourself just how beautiful you are. Tell yourself this morning that you love yourself, just as you are. Remember that you are special. Be true to yourself. Give yourself that special treat, you deserve it.*

Who are we kidding? We know what we actually deserve. Justice calls for an account. Love mandates change. Truth isn't found in isolated experience. Blood doesn't clean out from the carpet with just water. Reality is hard.

We aren't going to make this work on our own.

That is reality.

Once a misdeed falls from my bucket and lands in the holy waters of God's purpose, how can I pay for the waves that rise? I have trouble even considering how far those waves go. Even if I could see the full implications, what is the necessary cost for putting even the slightest wave in this perfect, holy purpose of God?

How detrimental is one act of unfaithfulness to an unconditional commitment? How dark is the contrast of one pencil line in an infinite sea of light? How many men and women, living broken lives, have given all they have for a good ideal? Over fifty million died in WWII, struggling against the ideals of fascism.[2] If this is the cost to preserve one set of ideals, how much, then, would a perfect purpose be worth?

It seems that, at least, this cost would be worth more than my life. It is possible the cost could never be counted. We can't unmake wrong. We can't pull back waves. We could never pay the cost.

God draws near. He is holy and loving, but in the land of reason, that statement has lost much of its comfort. What will happen if we see Him? What would happen if we could see ourselves rightly, if we see what we have actually become, what we have actually done in spite of God's love?

The situation indicates desperation, not victory. We have a cost we cannot pay, a burden we cannot shoulder. We've driven up the debt on our lives until it has become impossible for us to break even, and we owe it to the King of all joy, happiness, and love. Maybe you feel the weight, crushing down, making this hard to take in. I'll tell you the truth, you won't make it out of this mess on your own.

We must stake our hope in God's purpose for us.

We must stake our hope in Kingly love.

The result will be commitment and the changing of our lives.

In this respect, we find a major difference in the Agency of Origins and the agency of man. As Plato saw, "man is the son of poverty".[3] We need, and we need much. God needs nothing, and gives all.

Our judgment against the Standard is necessary for good and evil to exist at all. The ancient texts of the Bible demonstrate this problem quite clearly and propose a solution. God would shoulder the agency of people, not to eliminate agency, but to wipe the slate clean. God would choose to draw near, to *enter in*, so that he could stand in our place for the accounting. God would intervene, at great cost to Himself.

It is completely outrageous. Why would He do that?

There can be only one reason. He loves us, according to the real definition of love. Reason and love cross paths, they are nailed together in a miracle of God's good purpose. This is what He is like. We see it everywhere around us, when we look closely enough, whispers of what His Agency is like.

How can I summarize this story of hope? In one sense, I don't have to, it's already been summarized.[4] It is the story of a rescue, the story of a King and a lover, doing anything and everything to save a beloved.[5] God draws near, and changes the fabric of creation by instituting a new element of reality.

Grace.

Physics makes one thing clear: once you step into the chaotic world of time and space, you become entangled with it. It is one thing to suggest God is the

Agent of beginnings, and quite another to claim God *entered in*.

The characteristic trait of quantum physics is a conclusion called entanglement. Entanglement is an observation that two objects, even separated at great distances, can become entangled with the other. They no longer function independently, even though they are separated by space and time. Of course, the paradox demonstrated by entanglement is that it is not possible for information to be transferred faster than the speed of light (much less translated into action) between two objects that lay far apart...unless there is something else at work that can supersede time and space.

Einstein famously termed this, "spooky action at a distance," and assumed that the math of general relativity was incomplete or in error.[6] As it turned out (demonstrated in 2015), the math wasn't wrong.[7] This actually is how reality works.

What would it look like for the Agent of Origins (by definition exterior to space and time) to enter *into* time and space? To become entangled in the human condition, and all the suffering that goes with it? By doing so, the very nature of ourselves would become inseparable and entangled with His.

The texts of the Biblical story defy expectations and start to make logical sense. If God's purpose is good, and it is His purpose to draw near to us (and us to Him), there is little more He could do than become entangled in our condition. For justice to be done to humanity, it must be humanity who is judged. Yet who could bear the burden and right the sheer weight of wrongs, other than God?

Logically, if God entangled himself with us on our behalf, it would be an event within real human history, occurring at a specific time.[8] It would have to occur within a particular people and nation. Being entangled as a human, He would have to experience that universal human condition: death. Yet, being God, death would hold no power over Him. Being human, He would live and breathe in the brokenness of mankind. Yet, He would be impervious to it – and it would be as obvious as a light in the dark. It is unlikely this would look exactly like we might anticipate, yet it would change the course of the world. The brokenness of man would touch Him, become entangled, and be remade.

God becomes like us, to pay the cost. Once done, it would become history, another part of reality. Suddenly, it would not just be our actions that would matter. Our actions would be entangled with His ultimate action.

What would happen if this King bent His knee to His own creation? Physics tells us. He would become intimately entangled, inseparable, from that which He has entered; combining infinity and time into a paradox of life that exists both in the here and now, and forever into eternity.

It would open a door back to full life, to the beginnings of *very good*.

Love hopes it is true. Reason suggests it is necessary. Physics says it can happen.

Did it happen?

You must decide who Jesus of Nazareth is. As Lewis correctly pointed out, Jesus left us no middle ground. This Man is either a lunatic – on a level with the man who says he is a poached egg, or the Lord Himself, the King entangled in the human condition.[9] As you look closely, this Man is both beautiful and terrifying. His love is like fire, his mercies like snow, his judgment like steel.

Jesus was a Nazarene, a living man at a time in history. His living seems Divine, a picture of humility, love, and reason married perfectly together in power. His life is claimed to be the price of our agency's choice against God, a price that only God could pay. Roman, Jewish, and Christian history records that He paid, with willing suffering, rejection, lashes, and death. Death could not restrain His purpose.[10] Such trauma seemed to hold no power over Him, as if He was the source of all goodness and purpose.

By entangling himself in suffering, He would make our suffering bend its knee to His purpose.

We have retained our agency, but we are entangled with God. Though it has cost Him much, we can still ignore it. It is free to accept, and free to reject.

If we are to heal from our trauma, we must see His face. Then, we must fall in love. This will create commitment to a King who is worthy of all we can offer. This brings victory.

Let those who fear the Lord say,
"His steadfast love endures forever."

Out of my distress I called on the Lord;
the Lord answered me and set me free.
The Lord is on my side; I will not fear.
What can man do to me?
The Lord is on my side as my helper;
I shall look in triumph on those who hate me.

It is better to take refuge in the Lord
than to trust in man.
It is better to take refuge in the Lord
than to trust in princes.

I was pushed hard, so that I was falling,
but the Lord helped me.

The Lord is my strength and my song;
He has become my salvation.
Glad songs of salvation
are in the tents of the righteous:
"The right hand of the Lord does valiantly,
the right hand of the Lord exalts,
the right hand of the Lord does valiantly!"

I shall not die, but I shall live,
and recount the deeds of the Lord.
The Lord has disciplined me severely,
but He has not given me over to death.

Open to me the gates of righteousness,
that I may enter through them
and give thanks to the Lord.
This is the gate of the Lord;

the righteous shall enter through it.
I thank you that you have answered me
and have become my salvation.
The stone that the builders rejected
has become the cornerstone.
This is the Lord's doing;
it is marvelous in our eyes.
This is the day that the Lord has made;
let us rejoice and be glad in it.

- Psalm 118

What We Learned in this Chapter:

Reason only gets us so far. Love must come next, and love creates commitment. We must learn to love, and we can only do that if we see ourselves rightly. When we see ourselves rightly, we don't see much good. Reality is hard and, if we lean on reason alone, the situation seems desperate.

Love prompts us to call for help. God answers.

His answer is redemption. Redemption is God entangling Himself in our condition. To avoid contradiction, justice is necessary in reality. In love, God knew we couldn't understand (or pay) the cost. Only He could.

Therefore, God entangled himself within our consequences, taking our repercussions and producing something new in reality: Grace. This grace would be free, but it would cost. A lot. It would require God to become entangled in the full weight of human's self-induced suffering, and undergo the penalty: death. Yet, being God, it would have no power over Him.

We must decide who Jesus of Nazareth is. He is either a madman, or the Entangled Agent of Origins. He leaves us no middle ground. We can accept Him as King, or strike out on our own. We must decide.

We will love Him, hate Him, or accept confusion as our reality.

Come, let us return to the Lord;
for he has torn us, that he may heal us;
he has struck us down, and he will bind us up.

After two days he will revive us;
on the third day he will raise us up,
that we may live before him.

Hosea 6

Chapter Eight Notes

[1] A. W. Tozer, *The Knowledge of the Holy*. United Kingdom: James Clark & Co, 1965.

[2] Data from the Defense Casualty Analysis System.

[3] Plato, *The Symposium*.

[4] The Bible.

[5] To brush the dust off this story, I recommend *The Paradise King* by Blaine Eldredge.

[6] Einstein, Albert; Podolsky, Boris; Rosen, Nathan, *Can Quantum-Mechanical Description of Physical Reality Be Considered Complete?* Phys, 1935.

[7] Ronald Hanson, *Loophole-free Bell inequality violation using electron spins separated by 1.3 kilometres*. Nature, 2015, 526 (7575): 682–686.

[8] Note that the concept of time requires both external and internal observers.

[9] C. S. Lewis, *Mere Christianity*. New York: Macmillan, 1960.

[10] For a compilation of Roman, Jewish, and Christian historical sources, and an exceptionally well-written logical analysis of these events, I recommend the skeptic Frank Morison's book, *Who Moved the Stone?*

Chapter Ten

Tactics for Living Well 1.0

This is God's story and ours. We are entangled. He has made His choice, and it has been *very good*. Now, it is our turn. Nothing in what God has done has changed our agency. Nothing we have done has changed this King's providential purpose for reality. Therefore, a choice still lies before us: to live well, or not. To love Him, or not. To commit to His reality, or not.

Your allegiance will be somewhere. Will it be to this King? Or will it be toward your own agency, your own purposes, power, and choices?

This decision will change how you suffer, recover, and live.

At this point, a tactical approach is necessary. Tactics are different from rules. Tactics are strategies taught by another (or learned through experience), that assist in accomplishing an objective. Without tactics, the objective is still possible to achieve, but it is like swimming in full gear. Sinking is expected. A person who doesn't keep the rules gets in trouble. A person who doesn't use tactics is ignorant, and will learn the hard way.

Grace is free, it doesn't require anything except trust. However, the cost of grace was high and we cannot act in ignorance of that cost. Therefore, we have a responsibility. It is a responsibility to live well.

It will require tactics.

Recovering from trauma is one thing. Preventing it by living well, without regrets of action or inaction, is another. Living well requires training, discipline, and commitment – especially at first, when the ingrained habits of generations (and perhaps other principalities) fight for position and authority in our lives.

We need a teacher who speaks with Authority.

We need a teacher who is *Very Good*.

We have one.

From Matthew 5:1-16
In seeing the crowds, Jesus withdrew upon a mountain and sat down. His disciples came to Him, and he began to teach them...

Our first tactical lesson is the most important: We keep our eyes on Jesus and sit at His feet. It is within hard reality that Jesus sits down, an ancient posture of authority and openness. It is the teacher's position, kind but firm.

Are you keeping your eyes on Jesus, or on something else? He will revisit this teaching repeatedly: we cannot serve two masters. Where is your allegiance? Whom is it that you serve? What are you enslaved to? What can't you do without?

It is one thing to keep our eyes on Jesus, and another to sit at His feet. The western world is dominated by busy and, as Richard Foster reminds in his book *The Celebration of Discipline*, "Hurry isn't of the Devil, it is the Devil."[1] Again, Jesus warns us that remaining at His feet is the most central issue at stake in reality. Many will come in those last days saying, "Did we not prophesy in your name, cast out demons in your name, and work many wonders in your name?" His reply to them? "I will tell them: away from me, evil-doers. I never knew you."[2]

You can't get to know someone without learning to hear their voice, taking walks with them, calling them up for guidance and counsel. We *learn* to love people. We learn to love Jesus.

So, instead of fitting Jesus into your life (which is today), plan your life around Him. Use your agency to choose Him first, and everything else second. Yes, even family (bring them with you!). Even work. Even security. Even safety. All these things come after sitting at His feet. Francis Chan, in his book *Letters to the Church* suggests that if you aren't specifically setting aside time to pray at least an hour a day, you're not even giving Him as much time as you spend eating.[3] Peter of Celles notes that, "He who snores in the night of vice cannot know the light of contemplation."

Tactic 1.1: Sit at the feet of Jesus.

He began to teach them saying: Blessed are the poor in spirit, for theirs is the Kingdom of Heaven. Blessed are those who mourn, for they will be comforted. Blessed are the meek, for they will inherit the earth.

Jesus wastes no time with a lengthy introduction. He doesn't offer supporting evidence for His Authority. He doesn't need it, and He knows it. He immediately begins teaching on what life is full of: trauma, experiences that don't align with His good purpose.

He reaches people right in the midst of trauma and calls them to see His good purpose. Instead of recommending rigorous internal strength, or a prideful self-reliance, he teaches us to be humble. For those already broken, mourning, and meek, He makes a promise. The Kingdom of Heaven is near, much nearer than you might think. In the emptiness of grief, in the open space of humility, the world becomes still and we can hear His voice. Trauma does not have to be the conclusion; it can be a threshold into salvation. It is quite a promise.

He suggests that nothing should possess you except a desire, a hunger and thirst, for God's righteousness. When the chains of false reality fade and you grasp nothing except the hope in Christ as King, you will find that you have gained everything necessary for life.

What are you refusing to give to Him, holding onto because you think you 'need' it? Is it your strength? Your academic credentials? Your position of influence? Watchman Nee, in *The Normal Christian Life,* shares the applicable story of a man so dedicated to getting his doctorate degree that everything else was secondary, even following God. It wasn't until this man laid this agenda down at the feet of Jesus that he found peace and freedom.[4]

Jesus teaches us knowing that trauma is the natural result of a person grasping desperately onto things that don't bring life. He teaches us to let go, and hang singularly onto Him and His good purpose.

Tactic 1.2: Possess Jesus. Everything else will possess you.

Blessed are those who hunger and thirst for righteousness, for they will be filled. Blessed are the merciful, for they will be shown mercy. Blessed are the pure in heart, for they will see God.

After directly addressing the traumatized, he continues with our next tactic: how to have a full life. How are we supposed to know His will and what He is leading us toward? The answer has two parts. The first is desire. We must *desire* to know and do what is right. As we desire this, our consciousness will awaken. The King will draw near. Then, we must purify our hearts. We must choose to cast away evil from ourselves. The result is that we will see God. This teaching is completely counter to the eastern "empty yourself" methodology. We aren't trying to empty ourselves. We are trying, desiring, to fill ourselves with God's good purpose.

Sandwiched in the middle of this teaching is a

lesson on mercy. Mercy can only come about when you have been wronged and have the power to take action against the agency who has wronged you. It is almost as if Jesus is giving us a hint, or perhaps warning, about what it will look like when we hunger for righteousness and long to see God. The result will not look like a revenge fantasy. It won't look like constant self-justification. The natural outflow of righteousness and purity of heart will be mercy.

Our actions will start to look like the actions of Jesus.

Mercy requires more than kindness. It requires an understanding of yourself, the depth of your agency and, therefore, the knowledge that even your smallest mistakes have cost God greatly. Knowing where you stand in relation to God's purpose makes *us* rely on mercy. When we do, it becomes easier for us to give mercy to others.

As Dietrich Bonhoeffer says in *The Cost of Discipleship*, "...[these followers of Jesus] have renounced their own dignity, for they are merciful. As if their own needs and their own distress were not enough, they take upon themselves the distress and humiliation of others. They have an irresistible love for the down-trodden, the sick, the wretched, the wronged, the outcast, and all who are tortured with anxiety. They go out and seek all who are enmeshed in the toils of sin and guilt. No distress is too great, no sin too appalling for their pity. If any man falls into disgrace, the merciful will sacrifice their own honor to shield him, and take his shame upon themselves."[5]

Tactic 1.3: Want to know His will. If you want to

know His will, you will take tangible steps to cast away evil. Your barometer is your mercy.

Blessed are the peacemakers, for they will be called the sons of God. Blessed are those who are persecuted for the sake of righteousness, for theirs is the kingdom of heaven. And blessed are you when others hate you, revile you, and speak all kinds of evil against you because of me. Rejoice and be glad, for in the same way they persecuted the prophets who came before you.

Jesus ends His beatitude teachings with a firm warning: He is coming to demonstrate grace and life to those who seek after Him. He is doing nothing to restrict the agency God has given man. He is not changing the rules. He is fulfilling them.

Therefore, people can and will still choose to love what is evil. People will abandon logic, undermine the existence of right and wrong, kill their conscience, and shut off their touch of God's good purpose. They will be allied to their own power, instead of submitting to the Agency. The result will be more of what we know, more of what has been: trauma, pain, brokenness from evil, and the resulting collateral damage upon others. Such is the power of our agency.

Our task in these dark times is to be a peacemaker. A peacemaker sees God's purpose in ages past and traces that line into the future. A peacemaker does not self-isolate and build bunkers, focused on the small space around himself. A peacemaker is not a pacifist (one who refuses to fight). Nor does a peacemaker long for blood. A peacemaker is an agent who uses power in line with God's good purpose. Lewis states it well in his essay, *Why I am not a Pacifist*, "I think the art of life consists in tackling each immediate evil as well as we can. To avert or postpone one particular war by wise policy, or to render one particular campaign shorter by strength and skill or less terribly by mercy to the conquered and the civilians is more useful than all the proposals for universal peace that have ever been made; just as the dentist who can stop one toothache has deserved better of humanity than all the men who think they have some scheme for producing a perfectly healthy race."

A peacemaker is merciful, but not a fool. A peacemaker is a hostage negotiator in dark days, one who patiently reaches out a hand, while the other rests firmly on the hilt of the sword. The banner of mercy and the sword are both necessary tools in the hand of the peacemaker.

Jesus tells us not to despair at this dark future. On the contrary, He turns His back on mourning and commands, rejoice! Be glad in that day! Such is our trust in God's good purpose. Nothing can thwart His Agency. When all others turn aside from what is right, when they are uncomfortable because of your objective view of the world, and even when they hate you because of your commitment to the love and life of God, it is *very good*. It is in those dark moments and days that the light will shine the brightest.

Tactic 1.4: Remember that the world is evil, but God has predestined this evil for our good. Act like you are immortal, not like you are focused on your own interests.

> *You are the salt of the earth. If the salt loses its saltiness, how can it be made salty again? It is good for nothing, except to be thrown out and trampled by men.*
> *You are the light of the world. A city on a hill cannot be hidden. Nor does one light a lamp and stick it under a bowl. No, it is set on its stand, so it can give light to everyone in the house. In the same way, let your good deeds shine before men, so that others may see them and give praise to your Father who is in heaven.*

In those dark days, we will know who is the real light. It will be obvious. When you are under stress, when you are forced to kill or be killed, what will others see? Will they see a child of God, standing knee-deep in a river of unquenchable purpose? Will they see the peacemaker in glory, a child of the Living God?

What will others see in you, on your worst day?

Can you lay hands on the one who tried to kill your child, and lift him up? Can you bear the sword to love your neighbors, and then kneel amongst the fallen and bind your enemies' wounds? Can you see God's purpose for them in you?

When you can, you will be an unquenchable light. You'll find the absence of trauma, a full life of purpose. Desire this to be you, hunger and thirst for righteousness, God can and will redeem you.

There is no alternative. In this day, there will be salt and there will be dirt. There will be light, and there will be darkness. Allow your deeds in these dark days to shine out! Lay hands on the dying, and pray for them. Ask them for the reasons they have, the purpose they hold. Drag them with you, victoriously into the light. No resistance will prevail against you, for you rest in God's good purpose.

"A thousand may fall at your side, ten thousand at your right hand, but it will not come near you. You will only look with your eyes and see the punishment of the wicked. Because you have made the Lord your refuge, the Most High your dwelling place..."
- Psalm 91

Tactic 1.5: Do not be ashamed of Jesus and His Kingship over your life. On those "worst days" there will be a tidal wave of purpose, a great light. It will come from you, if you rest in Him.

What We Learned in this Chapter:

Living well necessitates specific tactics. In contrast with rules (which are requirements), tactics are methodologies, strategies that enable you to be successful in accomplishing your objective.

Jesus teaches us five tactics (among many others) to live well:

Tactic 1.1: Sit at the feet of Jesus.
Tactic 1.2: Possess Jesus. Everything else will possess you.
Tactic 1.3: Want to know His will. If you want to know His will, you will take tangible steps to cast away evil. Your barometer is your mercy.
Tactic 1.4: Remember that the world is evil, but God has predestined this evil for our good. Act like you are immortal, not like you are focused on your own interests.
Tactic 1.5: Do not be ashamed of Jesus and His Kingship over your life. On those "worst days" there will be a tidal wave of purpose, a great light. It will come from you, if you rest in Him.

I find the late Eugene Peterson, and his extensive work translating this ancient Arabic narrative into modern English, extremely insightful. As he was apt to say, "I would love to discuss with you my interpretation of this text, after you spend a decade studying the language in question".[6] Here are Jesus' words translated through Peterson's understanding in *The*

Message. Ponder His words within the context of your trauma:

> *Arriving at a quiet place, Jesus sat down and taught his climbing companions. This is what he said:*
>
> *"You're blessed when you're at the end of your rope. With less of you there is more of God and his rule.*
>
> *"You're blessed when you feel you've lost what is most dear to you. Only then can you be embraced by the One most dear to you.*
>
> *"You're blessed when you're content with just who you are - no more, no less. That's the moment you find yourselves proud owners of everything that can't be bought.*
>
> *"You're blessed when you've worked up a good appetite for God. He's food and drink in the best meal you'll ever eat.*
>
> *"You're blessed when you care. At the moment of being 'care-full,' you find yourselves cared for.*
>
> *"You're blessed when you get your inside world - your mind and heart - put right. Then you can see God in the outside world.*
>
> *"You're blessed when you can show people how to cooperate instead of compete or fight. That's when you discover who you really are, and your place in God's family.*
>
> *"You're blessed when your commitment to God provokes persecution. The persecution drives you deeper into God's kingdom.*
>
> *"Not only that - count yourselves blessed every*

time people put you down or throw you out or speak lies about you to discredit me. What it means is that the truth is too close for comfort and they are uncomfortable. You can be glad when that happens - give a cheer, even! - for though they don't like it, I do! And all heaven applauds. And know that you are in good company. My prophets and witnesses have always gotten into this kind of trouble.
Let me tell you why you are here. You're here to be the salt-seasoning that brings out the God-flavors of the earth."

- Matthew 5:2-13

Chapter Ten Notes

[1] Richard Foster, *The Celebration of Discipline*. San Fransisco: Harper Collins, 2009.
[2] Matthew 7:22-23
[3] Francis Chan, *Letters to the Church*. Colorado Springs: David C. Cook, 2018.
[4] Watchman Nee, *The Normal Christian Life*. Pennsylvania: CLC Publications, 2009.
[5] Deitrich Bonhoffer, *The Cost of Discipleship*. London: SCM Press, 1959
[6] Winn Collier, *A Burning in My Bones: The Authorized Biography of Eugene H. Peterson, Translator of The Message*. Colorado Springs: Waterbrook, 2021.

Chapter Eleven

Tactics for Living Well 2.0

Over the course of two months, every one of my Strike Team members memorizes this discourse by Jesus (often called the Sermon on the Mount). They recite it to judges at their graduation to demonstrate that they have fulfilled their commitment to sit at the feet of Jesus. To die well, we must live well. To live well, we must sit at the Master's feet.

You could do it too. You should do it.

We should hang onto His every word and look.

Jesus has given us a life's worth of tactics to develop in our lives, but He is not one to leave any stone unturned. He draws us out, until every room has been emptied and refilled with His presence.

From Matthew 6:1-34
Be careful not to practice your righteousness in front of others to be seen by them. If you do, you will receive no reward from your Father in heaven.

The second part of the Sermon on the Mount

continues Jesus' tactical lessons with a stern warning. If you care more about what people think than what God thinks, you are on the wrong road.

I have always taken this warning as one that cuts both ways: when you *do* something to be seen by people and when you *don't* do something because you are embarrassed to be seen doing it. As Jesus says later, "Whoever is ashamed of Me and of My words, of him will the Son of Man be ashamed when He comes in His glory and the glory of the Father and of the holy angels."[1] The warning mirrors His "I never knew you" statements.

Thus, one loyal to the King must carefully balance the scales, never acting for the applause of men, but never hiding when God calls us to be salt and light. When we find that balance, the reward is full life.

This English word "reward" does not fully encompass the repeated Greek phrase used as Jesus speaks of this reciprocity (He repeats it over and over again in the next few paragraphs). This word is '*apodidōmi*'. It is a rich word that means to restore, to recompense, to fulfill a solemn promise, and repeatedly deliver. It isn't a quid pro quo. It is a promise of restoration from a King, who always keeps His word. "Come to me, all who are thirsty and heavy laden, and I will give you rest."

Tactical lesson 2.1: Serve the Lord. Crucify your ego, and He will restore you.

So when you give to the needy, do not announce it with trumpets, as the hypocrites do in the synagogues and on the streets, to be honored by others. Truly I tell you, they have received their reward in full. But when you give to the needy, do not let your left hand know what your right hand is doing, so that your giving may be in secret. Then your Father, who sees what is done in secret, will apodidōmi.

Immediately, the Lord makes a firm assertion: if you have the right heart-set, if you live the way He wants, you'll recognize that "your" stuff isn't yours at all. I heard a pastor once say that if you want to know a person's priorities, look at their bank account. How true this statement is, and Jesus knows how fierce the battle will be. He goes so far as to make it clear later in the Sermon on the Mount saying, "You cannot serve both God and money." Are you enslaved to your stuff? Could you lose all of that stuff tonight, and wake up joyful tomorrow?

The only way to avoid this trap is by not letting your possessions possess you. He has said this already. Now, He gives further practical application: you must steward the resources you have by giving them, investing them, back into the areas of the world where there is need. Lewis highlights this by noting that the only apparent standard on how much we ought to give is an evaluation of our self-security. If we aren't giving enough to be uncomfortable, then it likely isn't enough.[2]

An author whom I read long ago (and who I can't recall or find) once suggested a daily practice to assist with this directive: anytime someone compliments you on a material item, offer it to them as a gift. This is a worthy practice to gauge how much you hold onto your possessions, and how much hold your possessions have on you. In the same breath, remember not to be a fool. The gifts you give your kids, the painting my wife beautifully composed for my birthday, our needs for daily life…these have enormous value, and may not really be "yours" to give. We should not grieve those closest to us, nor abdicate our responsibility as a provider for our family. Do not mistake generosity as the final expression of allegiance. Simply ask, along with the psalmist, "Test me, O God, and know my heart. See if there is any offensive way in me, and lead me in the way everlasting."[3]

When He repeats Himself, we'd do best to pay close attention, and He repeats himself many times on this point: ensure all you do is for the Lord alone. Humility is the only right response in the heart. As soon as it becomes about you and the attention you get from others, you are on the wrong road.

Tactical lesson 2.2: Have generosity and wise stewardship characterize your living. If you can't give it, you can lose it, and you are enslaved to it.

> *And when you pray, do not be like the hypocrites, for they love to pray standing in the synagogues and on the street corners to be seen by others. Truly I tell you, they have received their reward in full. But when you pray, go into your room, close the door and pray to your Father, who is unseen. Then your Father, who sees what is done in secret, will reward you. And when you pray, do*

not keep on babbling like pagans, for they think they will be heard because of their many words. Do not be like them, for your Father knows what you need before you ask him.

Knowing how to approach the Agency of Origins is not a task to take lightly. Jesus assumes that, if we are living correctly, we will draw near to God, the unseen Agency. He gives us careful instructions. As Andrew Murrey writes in the classic, *With Christ in the School of Prayer*: "Though in its beginning's prayer is so simple that the feeblest child can pray, yet it is at the same time the highest and holiest work to which man can rise. It is a fellowship with the Unseen and Most Holy One. The powers of the eternal world have been placed at its disposal. It is the very essence of true religion, the channel of all blessing, the secret of power and life."[4]

This is what it is like to draw near to a good King, full of power. It is the task of children and adults, the weak and the strong. All, in that place, are humbled. All see themselves in that place rightly.

The Lord teaches us how to pray, and it is the simplest and most difficult of tasks. Prayer is not all about asking God for things. It is not at all about talking a lot. It isn't like a speech around the dinner table, or a ritual of practice. He knows what we need, and works out His purpose for our good.

At its start, prayer implies drawing near, humbling yourself, and listening.

Again, Jesus sternly warns us to know why and to whom we pray. Is it for the ears of men? Are our prayers a covert message to our neighbors and family, or are they spoken to the King? Jesus, teach us how to pray! He will.

Tactical lesson 2.3: Listen in prayer. Ask Jesus to teach you how to pray.

This, then, is how you should pray:
'Our Father in heaven, hallowed be your name, your kingdom come, your will be done, on earth as it is in heaven. Give us today an everlasting bread. And forgive us our debts, as we forgive those who trespass against us. And lead us not into temptation, but deliver us from evil.'

I often wonder if the Lord took several moments of listening silence before he taught the foundation of prayer.

The intimacy of prayer stands out first. We draw near to this Agency not just as the King, but as a good Father. A good father is gentle and firm, wise and patient, loyal and true, fierce...and yet gives good hugs. A good father knows what we do in our rooms when the door is shut, and knows what is best for us. To indicate that we should have this level of intimacy with God when we speak to Him, suggests a proper reflection of everything we know about God's wisdom, purpose, knowledge and power. This is immensely humbling. Do you speak with God naked and unashamed? You can and will, if you see the chain of reasoning dictated through reality.

Filling our hearts with Him and His purpose is the next step of prayer. His name, His kingdom, His will.

There isn't an elimination of our *agency*, but there is a reordering of *priority*. Prayer doesn't start with what we can do for God, or what God can do for us. It is an acknowledgement of who He is. It is allegiance.

I think Kenneth Bailey in his book, *Jesus Through Middle Eastern Eyes,* correctly re-translates the phrase commonly read as 'daily bread'.[5] It does not seem to mean a meeting of physical needs, but of spiritual ones. *Give us a wholeness*, the heart cries out, *that will never perish*, even in the toughest of times.

Listening to God requires us to know *how* He speaks. Logically, this is pretty simple to figure out. God operated through a physical form once in history, so the words He said at that time must be pretty important. Lectio Divina is the ancient form of placing yourself in the story of Jesus and hearing His words to you. It is a practice worth studying. Any actual "hearing" (vibrations in the air) in the present time from God would be rare indeed (a miracle), but as we know the Agency of Origins is still working out His purpose, it seems logical we may still be able to commune with Him.

Imagine what you would sound like if you had no body, and were communicating with another person. What would it be like? It would be awakening to One intent on revealing Himself through a tendril of thought that is not your own, a brushing up against *something else,* quickening the word of life in your ears. It would require quieting your own inner dialogue enough to hear it, and an opening of your mind to the majesty of God. Some might call this *imagination*, and while this western term implies fictional experience, we know the imagination is much more than that. The time-independent elements of quantum mechanics (resulting in theories such as retro-causality) insinuates that the human brain is capable (especially during the production of theta waves) of doing much more than we think. Have you ever met a person who had a dream that then happened? Perhaps you have?

We regularly use our imagination to picture real things we can't see, from atomic structures to wavelengths traveling through the air. Imagination isn't the right word for this, especially when we quiet our heart and allow God to speak. Perhaps 'the imagery in the mind' is a better description. I highly recommend spending enough time with Jesus to know His voice before you spend much effort here.

If you struggle to hear the voice of God, I have a tip. Confess the errors of your heart, mind, and actions first. If you struggle to find errors in your thinking and actions, this is even *more* important. Read through 2nd Timothy (chapter three) to help open your eyes to your shortcomings.

Or, ask someone close to you to identify your shortcomings. If they refuse, consider it a stern warning. They likely fear your response, and prefer your ignorance. They are willing to accept a fake reality, over dealing with your reaction. Confessing to God is necessary and good, but confessing these shortcomings to the King in the presence of another person will literally open up the floodgates of God's presence in your prayer. When we open the door, God enters.

Tactical lesson 2.4: Pray well. Prepare your heart to draw near to the Voice of a Good Father. Spend time with Jesus, listen, confess, be filled.

For if you forgive other people when they sin against you, your heavenly Father will also forgive you. But if you do not forgive others their sins, your Father will not forgive your sins.

Interestingly, Jesus hinges this entire teaching on prayer with forgiveness. Is He saying that if we can't humble ourself enough to forgive, nothing else in reality will work?

Without the humility to forgive, life falls apart.

Forgiveness is an interesting term. Like confession, I think it means much more than an internal state. It is an action-based term that requires our hands to get dirty. Forgiveness is the reflection of an ending state, not a process. Jesus puts forgiveness in the correct perspective: how you are forgiven by God is what forgiveness looks like. This doesn't happen because you deserve it, or earn it. *Grace* is a gift that costs God much. Forgiveness, then, may cost *you* much. The recipient may not deserve it or earn it, but you must give it. The alternative is to live in an incorrect reality, where the perception of yourself is too high, and the judgment you pass on others too weighty. The result of this false reality is burdensome trauma, a ball and chain instead of life.

Tactical lesson 2.5: Forgiveness is necessary for living well.

When you fast, do not look somber as the hypocrites do, for they disfigure their faces to show others they are fasting. Truly I tell you, they have received their reward in full. But when you fast, put oil on your head and wash your face, so that it will not be obvious to others that you are fasting, but only to your Father, who is unseen; and your Father, who sees what is done in secret, will reward you.

What do you think you can't live without? It is not surprising to me that most high-level combat teams (such as the Rangers) force their applicants to fast as part of their acceptance into the program. Fasting brings out what is deep within you, and (even when not done for God's purpose) helps you see what you can and can't live without.

Jesus assumes that the ancient discipline of fasting will be practiced as a matter of course.[6] You can fast from nearly anything, but I find the most costly and difficult to be what Jesus references here: fasting from food. Fasting from food causes a substantial disruption to your routine. It cuts into your agenda and gnaws at your emotions.

What comes out of your heart under stress? Is it anger or frustration? Laziness or contempt? Such things come from within you, not from being hungry. When you fast, are you proud of your accomplishment? Of how easy it is, or how disciplined you are? Fasting forces us to face both sides of pride within ourselves, and examine our inmost being for true humility and dependence on God's purpose.

Tactical lesson 2.6: Fast to increase your reliance on God's purpose. Fast to test your humility.

Do not store up for yourselves treasures on earth, where moths and vermin destroy, and where thieves break in and steal. But store up for yourselves treasures in heaven, where moths and vermin do not destroy, and where thieves do not break in and steal. For where your treasure is, there your heart will be also.

As if we haven't quite gotten the point, Jesus makes this repetitive lesson perfectly clear. What we value – be that the applause or approval of men, the comforts of security, or the fullness of God – will determine how we live and die. Jesus knows that if our heart trusts in anything that is not Himself, trauma will be the result. To live well, we must set our heart on God's purpose. Seeking this treasure with all our resources can be our only aim, for this treasure is the *real* treasure.

Tactical lesson 2.7: Treasure God, and victory will be guaranteed.

The eye is the lamp of the body. If your eyes are healthy, your whole body will be full of light. But if your eyes are unhealthy, your whole body will be full of darkness. If then the light within you is darkness, how great is that darkness!

Jesus turns his attention to a specific element of human behavior. Our eyes. Humans are extremely visual creatures. Research indicates that eighty to eighty-five percent of our learning, perception, and activities are facilitated through our vision.[7] What we spend time looking at changes who we are.

I define an addiction as anything that we *feel* we can't function or be normal without (but we really don't need). Addictions cause a well-studied effect in the brain: cerebral dysfunction. This means that the strategic areas of the brain begin to shut down, degrade, and ultimately disappear, resulting in impulsivity, emotional compulsivity, and impaired judgment. Interestingly, when a normal bodily process (like eating or sex) becomes an addiction (overeating and pornography), they have an identical negative effect on the brain as other major addictions (such as cocaine and meth).[8]

Do you know what else causes these same dysfunctional symptoms in the brain?

Trauma.

Addiction and trauma look the same in the brain. They are reflections of a false reality.

Are your eyes healthy? Are you enslaved to something in and of the world? Jesus poses this question and lays out the consequences. He knows exactly how humans function. He's right, of course. Today, the gross world pornography revenue exceeds that of Google, Apple, Netflix, Microsoft, and Amazon combined. As Watts points out in this compelling research, these industries claim that associating pornography as "bad" comes from religious and moral stigma, and promptly identify this as infringement of peoples 'rights'. You should notice how this argument doesn't make any logical sense, as "rights" are ethics based on moral values. Relativism serves those in power who stand to profit.

Apparently, we have a right to defy reality and destroy our humanity. God will let us, if we choose. The result will be a darkness so great it will consume our God-given humanity.

Tactical lesson 2.8: Identify all addiction in your life. Do everything necessary to cut them out completely. Replace addiction with devotion to God's purpose.

No one can serve two masters. Either you will hate the one and love the other, or you will be devoted to the one and despise the other. You cannot serve both God and money.

Whom do you serve?

Jesus speaks to the heavy laden, the suffering, and the enslaved. His audience is traumatized, we are traumatized, because we have taken our agency to the extreme. We have turned from life, from a reality that makes sense, to our own devices. Again and again, He tells us the cure: *return to My good purpose.*

It is impossible to love God *and* love those things that bind, that drag people away from His good purpose. Being devoted to one results in the detestment of the other. The word Jesus uses for hate (*miséō*) doesn't just involve strong feelings. It involves action. Miséō means to take a stand against these things, in your life and the lives of others.[9]

It means to fight against.

What must you fight against? What attempts to enslave you? What gnaws at your thoughts and grips at your heart? Jesus warns us that money, the god of providing for ourselves and making our own way, will be the leader in the pack among false, enslaving masters.

You must make your stand. Will it be with God's good purpose and against evil? Or will it be in a world of relativistic values, where each person can do whatever they want? There is no middle ground.

Tactical lesson 2.9: Devotion to God's purpose results in striving against those things that are evil.

Therefore I tell you, do not worry about your life, what you will eat or drink; or about your body, what you will wear. Is not life more than food, and the body more than clothes? Look at the birds of the air; they do not sow or reap or store away in barns, and yet your heavenly Father feeds them. Are you not more valuable than they? Can any one of you by worrying add a single hour to your life? And why do you worry about clothes? See how the flowers of the field grow. They do not labor or spin. Yet I tell you that not even Solomon in all his splendor was dressed like one of these. If that is how God clothes the grass of the field, which is here today and tomorrow is thrown into the fire, will he not much more clothe you—you of little faith?

So do not worry, saying, 'What shall we eat?' or 'What shall we drink?' or 'What shall we wear?' For the pagans run after all these things, and your heavenly Father knows that you need them. But seek first his kingdom and his righteousness, and all these things will be given to you as well. Therefore do not worry about tomorrow, for tomorrow will worry about itself. Each day has enough trouble of its own.

In my de-escalation classes, I teach that anxiety is a normal element of the human condition. Problems produce anxiety. This is the psychology of mankind at its most basic level. But it seems God disagrees. Anxiety is not natural in the human condition that He designed. Anxiety, then, is a by-product of our choices, the result of our abused agency.

When we trust God's purpose, worry disappears. Trauma vacates our lives. What remains is God. His kingdom, His righteousness, and a Promise. The promise is to you, it is the promise of a full life, a life redeemed, a life provided for. Trust His purpose and in this life, victory will be guaranteed.

Tactical lesson 3.0: Seeking out the reality of God's purpose, one day at a time, means that victory is guaranteed.

What We Learned in this Chapter:

There is great importance to know and apply the instructions Jesus gave us for how to live. Here are ten additional tactics:

Tactical lesson 2.1: Serve the Lord. Crucify your ego, and He will restore you.

Tactical lesson 2.2: Have generosity and wise stewardship characterize your living. If you can't give it, you can lose it, and you are enslaved to it.

Tactical lesson 2.3: Listen in prayer. Ask Jesus to teach you how to pray.

Tactical lesson 2.4: Pray well. Prepare your heart to draw near to the Voice of a Good Father. Spend time with Jesus, listen, confess, be filled.

Tactical lesson 2.5: Forgiveness is necessary for living well.

Tactical lesson 2.6: Fast to increase your reliance on God's purpose. Fast to test your humility.

Tactical lesson 2.7: Treasure God, and victory will be guaranteed.

Tactical lesson 2.8: Identify all addiction in your life. Do everything necessary to cut them out completely. Replace addiction with devotion to God's purpose.

Tactical lesson 2.9: Devotion to God's purpose results in striving against those things that are evil.

Tactical lesson 3.0: Seeking out the reality of God's purpose, one day at a time, means that victory is guaranteed.

Chapter Eleven Notes

[1] Matthew 7:23

[2] C. S. Lewis, *Mere Christianity*. New York: Macmillan, 1960.

[3] Psalm 139

[4] Andrew Murrey, *With Christ in the School of Prayer*. New York: Fleming H. Revell Company, 1895.

[5] Kenneth Bailey, *Jesus Through Middle Eastern Eyes*. Illinois: Intervarsity Press, 2009

[6] Foster's book, *The Celebration of Discipline,* is a valuable resource in learning how to practice many of the disciplines Jesus teaches.

[7] Thomas Politzer, O.D. Former NORA President, Neuro-Optometric Rehabilitation Association, 2018.

[8] C. Watts, *Pornography addiction: A neuroscience perspective*. Surg Neurol Int., 2011.

[9] Strong's Lexicon may be a useful tool for a serious student of the Bible's original languages.

Chapter Twelve

It's Personal

Trauma is always personal.

Recovery from trauma is a misnomer. Recovery doesn't exist. What does exist is a *new* normal, a new world. You can live in this new world. I hope it is a world that aligns with reality, the real reality of purpose and redemption. You must choose to see reality for what it is.

You know that trauma leaves no room for error.

When I teach about recovery from violence, I tell my secularized audience the truth: if you ask me a personal question, you should expect a personal answer. Of course, I know that personal questions are impossible to avoid when discussing violence.

So, when it is time to go deep, I give three recommendations.

I give them now to you.

First, walk down the road together. Don't go through dark times alone, and don't allow others to do so. Humans have a tendency to push others away and isolate when their world shatters and pain draws near. They are crying out, "Help me!" Can you hear it? What do you hear, when someone pushes you away with words and actions? Will you ignore these problems, because you have enough of your own? Or will you lean in?

I have a list of men and women who have walked down those dark paths with me. They were wise enough to know I needed them, even if I didn't want to accept their love. Melissa and Zach, Steve and Rebekah, John and Gavin and Duke. There are many more. Each helped me hobble forward and see myself and the world as it really was. Whom are you walking alongside? Who walks alongside you?

Second, learn how to tell your story. By telling it to others, you will begin to see a vein of purpose. You will begin to see that God can work out all things for your good. Telling your story won't be easy, especially when you peel back the layers of forgetfulness and lies you've compiled over the years. We have a tendency to bury pains in our heart, expecting time to heal them. Instead, we find that these wounds fester. Buried pain infects everything near it, like ink diffusing out in a radius of contamination. This poison seeps out into the waters of our lives, tainting surrounding memories, infecting near relationships, and changing how we live.

Share your story. Find those deep, dark places in your heart and open them up to fresh air. Let the light shine in. Confess what you have done, and what has been done to you. I tell you the truth, it may take years to learn how to share your story. I had to write my stories out at first, because I couldn't speak during the telling of them. My heart was like water, poured out upon the ground. The burdens were too great.

I have never stopped writing those stories. As you practice, share, and allow God to walk with you down those paths of history, you will find healing. He can heal the wounds of ages past, if you open up the doors and let Him in.

Finally, ask hard questions about reality and your life. By asking hard questions, you will discover what reality looks like. You will begin to see yourself rightly. It won't be easy, but it will be good. You will begin to see what God looks like, and as you sit at His feet you will see with greater clarity your part to play in the course of His purpose.

You may *feel* the burden to be too heavy, but I have found it to be quite light if you stand in the right. Our feelings, our addictions, and our opinions can lead us astray. Reason grounds us in reality. Love helps us enter further in.

Every link of the chain that anchors our reality must be sound.

This book has scratched the surface of those hard questions. There are more. Don't run from them. Lean in. Lean on His kindness, His good purpose. Ask a lot of questions and find answers that make sense. Help others to do the same. As you do, you'll fall in love, into the source of Love. It will be a love that satisfies like bread and crushed grapes, that refreshes like clean mountain air, and restores like sweet, deep sleep.

Remember, love leads us toward commitment.

Reason sets the foundation love must rest on. Together, reason and love lead us into allegiance.

You'll be amazed to find this love reciprocated, living and active, giving and binding, teaching and rebuking. He has come for you, and He will heal you.

Before long, the world will not see me anymore, but you will see me. Because I live, you also will live.
On that day you will realize that I am in my Father, and you are in me, and I am in you.
Abide in me, and I will abide in you.

- *The Prince of Peace*

What We Learned in this Chapter:

I give you three personal applications for trauma.

First, walk down the road together.
Second, tell your story – even (and especially) the hard parts.
Third, ask the hard questions.

We have asked some hard questions together. There are more to ask, answers for them exist. Lean into these questions. As you do, you will find yourself falling into Love, the source of love. Let this love rest on the bedrock of reason, and turn into allegiance. He has come for you, and He will heal you.

Finally, whatever is true, whatever is honorable, whatever is just, whatever is pure, whatever is lovely, whatever is commendable, if there is any excellence, if there is anything worthy of praise, think about these things.

- Philippians 4:8-9

If you are empowered by the message of this book and recognize a need to make a change, consider the following suggestions:
- Give this book to friends (or strangers) as a gift. You may impact a life as you share this glimpse into reality, not often presented in our culture.
- Share on a website, blog, or social media account how this compilation touched your life.
- Encourage your teachers in local schools or leaders in houses of worship to read this.
- Challenge a small group to evaluate this book together as a team.

Visit www.pacific-books.com to view other books by G. R. Burns.

If you have questions, comments, or a desire to learn more about the TTA Strike Team Program and other TTA resources, you can contact the TTA.

Tactical Training Academy
www.Training-Academy.org
info@Training-Academy.org

Made in the USA
Middletown, DE
08 May 2024